THE GOD-MEN

Witness Lee

Living Stream Ministry
Anaheim, CA

First Edition, June 1995.

ISBN 978-0-87083-871-2

Published by

Living Stream Ministry
2431 W. La Palma Ave., Anaheim, CA 92801 U.S.A.
P. O. Box 2121, Anaheim, CA 92814 U.S.A.

Printed in the United States of America

08 09 10 11 12 / 12 11 10 9 8 7 6 5

CONTENTS

PREFACE

This book is composed of messages given by Brother Witness Lee in Anaheim, California on May 26-29, 1995.

CHAPTER ONE

THE GOD-MEN AND THE NEW MAN

Scripture Reading: Eph. 2:15-16; 4:22-24; Col. 3:10-11

OUTLINE

I. The God-men:
   A. Born of God to be His sons—John 1:12-13; Heb. 2:10.
   B. Having the divine life—John 3:15, 36a.
   C. Having the divine nature—2 Pet. 1:4.
   D. Having two lives, human and divine, living together as one life.
   E. Having two natures, humanity and divinity.
   F. The human life (the old man) being crucified for the living of the divine life with the resurrected human life (the new man)—Gal. 2:20a; Eph. 4:22-24.
   G. For the manifestation of God in the flesh as the new man—1 Tim. 3:16; Eph. 2:15.
   H. Growing up for the purpose of building up the organic Body of Christ for the fulfillment of the eternal economy of God—Eph. 4:12-13, 15-16.

II. The new man:
   A. Created by Christ.
   B. With the Jews and the Gentiles as the materials.
   C. In Himself as the divine element—Eph. 2:15.
   D. Through His death on the cross.
   E. To be the one new man for the Body of Christ—Eph. 2:16.
   F. Having the believers as his constituents, who are Christ and in whom is Christ.
   G. To be the corporate Christ—Col. 3:10-11.

H. By the believers:
  1. Putting off the old man.
  2. Putting on the new man.
  3. Through the renewing of the spirit in their
     mind—Eph. 4:22-24.
I. To be the new creation of God:
  1. In Christ as the element—2 Cor. 5:17.
  2. As the unique accomplishment in God's econ-
     omy—Gal. 6:15:
     a. The New Jerusalem as the ultimate con-
        summation of God's divine work—Rev. 21:2:
        1) Through the four ages of humanity.
        2) By Himself in Christ and through the
           Spirit as the Triune God.
     b. Showing God's wisdom, as a shame to God's
        enemy Satan in his cosmos—Eph. 3:10.

Prayer: Lord, we thank You that by Your mercy and grace we can be here, gathered together into You. Lord, we believe that Your oracle will be here again. Speak to us. Open us to You as You are open to us. Lord, we need Your clear sky. Take away all the veils. We need to see something that is deep within You. We do not want knowledge; we do not want doctrine. We desire to touch Yourself as the life-giving Spirit, as the transforming Spirit, as the glorifying Spirit, as the Lord Spirit. We do not want to touch anything else. Hallelujah! You are such a Spirit, and You are now in our spirit. We thank You and worship You for these two spirits, the divine Spirit and the human spirit mingled together as one spirit. Tonight we believe that we are in this one spirit. Speak to us in this spirit. Even, Lord, speak in our speaking. Amen.

The burden for the messages in this book can be expressed in the following two sets of statements, the first set concerning the God-men (plural) and the second concerning a God-man (singular):

Set 1:

The God-men, as the regenerated children of God, constitute the new man, as the new creation of God, with the divine life.

The God-men, as the spiritual household of God, build up the Body of Christ, as the Triune God's organism, with the transforming life.

The God-men, as the royal priesthood of God, struggle to be the overcomers, as God's Zion in Jerusalem, with the reigning life.

The God-men, as the chosen race of God, consummate the New Jerusalem, as God's eternal expression, with the glorifying life.

Set 2:

A God-man who knows the excellent Christ should live a life conformed to the death of Christ by the power of His resurrection (Phil. 3:8, 10).

A God-man who has Christ living in him should live

Christ and magnify Christ by the bountiful supply of His Spirit (Gal. 2:20; Phil. 1:19-21).

A God-man who has been freed by Christ as the Lord Spirit should be transformed and conformed to the glorious image of Him as the firstborn Son of God (2 Cor. 3:17-18; Rom. 8:29).

To reign by grace in life in this age and to triumph in Christ unto glory in the next age.

The subject of the messages in this book can be expressed in just two words: the God-men. The six chapters of this book cover four major topics: the first, the God-men and the new man; the second, the God-men and the Body of Christ; the third, the God-men and the overcomers; and the last, the God-men and the New Jerusalem. The New Jerusalem is the conclusion of the entire sixty-six books of the Bible.

Some may ask, "In what book, what chapter, and what verse can you find this wonderful term *the God-men?*" The answer is very simple. Although we cannot find the term *the Triune God* in the Bible, nearly all Bible students recognize that the entire Bible reveals the Triune God. In the same principle, although we cannot find the term *the God-men* in the Bible, the fact, the reality, of the God-men is in the Bible. Initially, the Bible speaks of the God-man. Today this God-man has become the God-men. The God-man is Jesus Christ, who is God incarnated to be a man. As such a One, He is the God-man. Furthermore, He is the model God-man, the prototype for the producing of many God-men (Rom. 1:3-4; 8:29), including all the dear saints throughout the world. Regardless of our nationality, and regardless of whether we are male or female, young or old, we all must believe that we are God-men. We are all God-men, and each one of us is a God-man.

I. THE GOD-MEN

A. Born of God to Be His Sons

The first qualification of the God-men is that they are born of God to be His many sons (John 1:12-13; Heb. 2:10). Originally, we were merely created men. After being created, we became fallen sinners. We were not sons of God. But praise Him, according to His eternal economy, four thousand years after He created Adam, God came out of eternity and entered into time, and He became a man. This man is Jesus Christ. In the past two thousand years of human history, Jesus Christ as the God-man has influenced the entire world. Today He is still doing the same thing, but He is doing it not by Himself alone but by thousands and even millions of God-men, who are the mass reproduction of Him as the prototype.

Although we are of different races and nationalities, by His mercy we have all become the same: we are all God-men. A God-man is one who has been born of God. In Christianity there is a theology that tells people that we believers became sons of God not by birth but by adoption. According to this theology, we were not born of God but were merely adopted by God. However, according to the Scriptures, we, the believers in Christ, were all born of God to be His sons. As the sons of God, surely we are God-men. We are the same as the One of whom we were born. It would be impossible to be born of God and not be the sons of God. Since we are the sons of God, we are God-men.

B. Having the Divine Life

As sons of God and as God-men, we have the divine life (John 3:15, 36a). Many Christians realize that they have eternal life, yet they do not know what eternal life is. Furthermore, they do not know what the divine life is. They do not know that, as regenerated ones, they have another life in addition to their own human life. We all need to realize that in addition to our natural life, we have another life, the divine life. The natural life makes us a natural man, and the divine life makes us a divine man. We all can boast that we are divine persons because we have been born of the divine life. Since we have been born of the divine life and possess the divine life, surely we are divine persons. We have been born of the divine life; therefore, we are divine. It is a pity that the majority of regenerated people do not know that they have God's life in addition to their own life. Our own life is a human life; thus, we are all human. But through regeneration we have received another life, which has been added to our natural life. This life is not only holy and heavenly but also divine. Thus, we have all become divine.

Although we are divine men, we need to ask ourselves whether we live, act, and behave ourselves as divine men. Some of us may feel that we are not qualified to be even a human man, not to mention a divine man. Because of our poor behavior, we may consider ourselves "turtles" and not men. Nevertheless, because we have been born of God and have the divine life, we can say that we are not only higher than the turtles, but we are even much higher than the top human beings. We may feel that we are not qualified to say this, but actually we are more than qualified. My burden in these messages is to help you to see a vision from the heavens. Do not look at yourself. We are not worthwhile to look at. We must look away to the heavens. In the heavens the angels are rejoicing because they see that all the believers are divine. The angels have only the angelic life; they are not divine. What an honor and what a glory that we human beings can be divine!

In our recent crystallization-study of the Epistle of James, I pointed out that the Christian perfection stressed by James is not the genuine Christian perfection revealed in the entire divine revelation of the New Testament. I said that the perfection stressed by James is a pretense and is the product of self-cultivation, by the natural life endeavoring to develop the "bright virtue" in the man of the old creation. This is in contrast with the genuine Christian perfection, which is produced by the believers with the rich element of all that Christ is, by the bountiful supply of the all-inclusive consummated Spirit, and through the power of Christ's resurrection and the death of Christ's cross. The Bible, according to God's economy, teaches all God's chosen ones, who have believed in Christ and have been regenerated by the Spirit and who have become the God-men, to be divine persons (Gal. 2:20; Phil. 1:19-21a).

C. Having the Divine Nature

As those who are born of God, the God-men have not only the divine life but also the divine nature. Thank God that in the Bible, among the sixty-six books, there is one verse, 2 Peter 1:4, that says that we are partakers of the divine nature, which is the nature of God. We should mark such a verse in our Bibles so that whenever we open the Bible, that verse will stand out. We are not turtles, because we do not have the turtle nature. We are men, for we do have the human nature. But we have also been born of God; we are God's sons, God's children. Thus, we have God's nature. Since we have God's nature, are we not God? In fact, we are God in His life and His nature, but not in His Godhead.

D. Having Two Lives, Human and Divine, Living Together as One Life

As God-men, we also have two lives, human and divine, living together as one life. We may wonder how two lives could live together as one life. The answer is very simple. In grafting, a branch from one tree is grafted into another tree. The two are joined together, and the two lives live together as one life. In the same principle, we, the believers, have been grafted into Christ (Rom. 11:17-19) and are living in an organic union with Him. In such a union the human life and the divine life are joined as one so that they live together as one mingled life and one living.

E. Having Two Natures, Humanity and Divinity

The God-men not only have two lives, but they also have two natures, humanity and divinity. This is marvelous. Today's Christianity makes God's salvation merely a religion. Religion does not teach people to be God-men by receiving God into them. Religion always cultivates man's natural capacity in order to build up the self. Education does the same thing; it merely builds up the human being. Apparently, the Bible also does this, but actually it does not. The Bible does not build up the natural man; rather, it builds up a God-man. We are born of God, and we are children of God. The Bible builds us up to be proper God-men.

My burden in the Lord's ministry is not to build you up to be a nice man, a good man, or a gentle man, but to be a

God-man. I have given thousands of messages on how to be a
Christ-man, a God-man. In the Lord's recovery our teaching
is not to raise up good men. Our teaching, absolutely according to the Bible, is to raise up God-men.

Eventually, the Bible builds up a corporate man. Ultimately,
this corporate man will be enlarged to be its consummation,
the New Jerusalem. The issue of the Bible's teaching is just
one entity, the New Jerusalem as the aggregate of all the
God-men.

We need to know by seeing that we have God's life and
possess God's nature. There is such a fact that the divine life
is mingled with our human life. Therefore, we must learn how
to live not by our human life but by God's life mingling with
our human life to make us divine.

F. The Human Life (the Old Man) Being
Crucified for the Living of the Divine Life with
the Resurrected Human Life (the New Man)

Our human life (the old man) has been crucified for the
living of the divine life with the resurrected human life
(the new man) (Gal. 2:20a; Eph. 4:22-24). Our old man, the
natural man, should not be cultivated. Rather, it should be
cut off; it should be crucified. It has been crucified already
with Christ on the cross (Rom. 6:6). Christ has crucified all
His believers so that His believers may live not by the crucified life but by the divine life in a humanity that is
resurrected. Now the divine life is living not in the natural
humanity but in the resurrected humanity. That is the new
man. We all need to see such a vision. Because I have seen
this, I always hate my own humility. I hate my humility much
more than my pride, because both my pride and my humility
belong to the old man. We should always be reminded that
our old man was crucified. Then, in regeneration our natural
humanity was resurrected. Regeneration is a resurrection (cf.
Acts 13:33). To be regenerated is to be resurrected with the
divine life. Therefore, today we should live a life conformed to
the death of Christ (Phil. 3:10) that the divine life may have
an opportunity to live with our resurrected humanity.

G. For the Manifestation of God
in the Flesh as the New Man

This is for the manifestation of God in the flesh as the new man (1 Tim. 3:16; Eph. 2:15). First Timothy 3:16 says, "And confessedly, great is the mystery of godliness: He who was manifested in the flesh." According to the context of this verse, godliness here refers not only to piety but also to the living of God in the church, that is, to God as life lived out in the church. Godliness means that God becomes man and man becomes God. This is a great mystery in the universe. God has become man so that man may become God to produce a corporate God-man for the manifestation of God in the flesh as the new man.

H. Growing Up for the Purpose of Building Up
the Organic Body of Christ for the Fulfillment
of the Eternal Economy of God

This corporate God-man grows up for the purpose of building up the organic Body of Christ for the fulfillment of the eternal economy of God (Eph. 4:12-13, 15-16). The manifestation of God is possible by the Body of Christ. The Body of Christ is just the manifestation of God for the fulfillment of the eternal economy of God. Regardless of how much our natural self can be built up, and regardless of how much our natural capacity can be cultivated, we can never be the manifestation of God, and we can never be a part of the Body of Christ. This must be the responsibility of the God-men. The God-men are born of God to have God's life and God's nature, to live by a mingled life in a mingled nature, to build up the Body of Christ as God's manifestation. This is the revelation of the Bible. The natural concept we have received from human philosophy and religion is not the revelation of the Bible. The Bible does not teach this. The Bible teaches that a man must be born of God to be a God-man, and this God-man must be raised up, must grow up. Then the God-men know how to build up themselves to be the Body of Christ for the manifestation of God and for the fulfillment of God's economy.

II. THE NEW MAN

The Bible never says that there are many new men. The Bible tells us that there is only one new man (Eph. 2:15). This one new man is not an individual; he is a corporate man, and this corporate new man is the aggregate of all the God-men. When we put all the God-men together, we have one man. This one man is called "the new man" (Eph. 4:24; Col. 3:10), referring to the new mankind. Adam was the old mankind. All his descendants are one with him to be the old man. Today we, the believers in Christ, are all one with Christ to be the new man.

A. Created by Christ

The new man was created by Christ (Eph. 2:15). To understand how the new man was created, we need a detailed definition. We were born the old man. One day we heard about the Lord Jesus and we believed in Him, and we received Him into us. He is the very embodiment of God (Col. 2:9). This means that when the Lord Jesus entered into us, God came into us; God was imparted into us. On the one hand, the divine element was brought into our being, and on the other hand, Christ terminated our old nature on the cross. Hence, Christ terminated our old nature and imparted God into us as the new element. By these two things Christ created us to be the new man. To create us, the sinners, to be the new man, our natural person, our natural being, had to be crossed out, and God Himself had to be imparted into us. This is the constitution of the new man.

B. With the Jews and the Gentiles as the Materials

According to Ephesians 2:15, Christ used the Jews and the Gentiles as the materials in His creating of the new man. Christ created the new man by imparting the divine nature into the redeemed humanity of the believing Jews and Gentiles.

C. In Himself as the Divine Element

Ephesians 2:15 says, "...that He [Christ] might create the

two in Himself into one new man." The new man was created in Christ as the divine element. When we were the old man, we had the human element but did not have the divine element. Since God Himself has been imparted and added into us, we now have the divine element in us. Since we have the divine element, we have become something new. This new thing in its totality is the new man.

D. Through His Death on the Cross

The new man was created through Christ's death on the cross. Thousands of Christians have read Ephesians 2:15; 4:24; and Colossians 3:10, and they have seen the term *the new man* according to the letter, but they do not know what the new man is. Our becoming the new man was not merely a matter of our repenting and being sorry for our past and thereby becoming new. This is the teaching of Confucius; it is not the teaching of the Bible. In the creating of the new man, first our natural man was crucified by Christ on the cross, and then through the crossing out of the old man, Christ imparted God's element into us. Thus, we became an entity that is different from the old man, because we have God's element in us.

Ephesians 2:15 tells us that Christ did this creating work on the cross. We usually consider that Christ's work on the cross was related only to negative things, to cross us out, to crucify us. But Ephesians 2:15 tells us that on the cross Christ did something positive, to generate us, not to put us to death. This divine thought is clearly seen in Ephesians 2:15. The cross of Christ not only destroys and kills; it also generates and brings in something divine.

The new man was created by Christ with two kinds of materials. The first is the redeemed created man; the second is the divine element. On the cross Christ put these two materials together to produce a new man. If a grain of wheat is sown into the earth, on the one hand the grain of wheat will die. While it is dying, it is growing. The death of the grain of wheat brings forth a new plant. What was once only a grain of wheat eventually becomes a new plant that bears many grains of wheat (John 12:24). Through the death of the grain of wheat, the grain of wheat is terminated. At the same time, something is germinated that grows up to be a new plant. This is an illustration of what was accomplished in Christ's death. While He was on the cross, Christ was terminating, and He was also begetting.

First Peter 1:3 says that God the Father begot us through Christ's resurrection. According to this view, we were crucified on the cross and were germinated in Christ's resurrection. Thus, it may seem incorrect to say that Christ begot us on the cross. However, we should never separate resurrection from the cross. Christ's death is always linked to His resurrection. His death brings in resurrection. In John 12:24 the Lord Jesus said, "Unless the grain of wheat falls into the ground and dies, it abides alone; but if it dies, it bears much fruit." The one grain of wheat falls into the earth to die, but this death causes the grain to grow and become a hundred grains of wheat. In the death of the one grain we can see two things: the dying of the grain of wheat and the bringing forth of a new life. Similarly, when we receive Christ into us as our Savior and life, He is always with His death and resurrection.

Furthermore, the Lord's resurrection includes His death. His death power is implied and included in His resurrection. His resurrection cannot be separated from His death. When we receive Him as our life, that life is resurrection (John 11:25), and in that life there is also the element of death. On the one hand, it imparts life to us, and at the same time, it crucifies us. Therefore, to be a believer as a God-man is not to cultivate anything of our natural life. We must realize that we have received Christ as our life (Col. 3:4a), and this life is in resurrection. Moreover, in that resurrection there is continually a putting to death.

We all know from our experience that the more we pray to the Lord, the more we contact the Lord, the more we allow the Lord to impart Himself into us, on the one hand, the more we become spiritually alive, and on the other hand, the more we desire to terminate our old self. After our proper prayer, the issue is always that we become living and at the same time are put to death. This kind of experience produces the new man. The Bible tells us in Ephesians 2:15 that Christ created the Jews and the Gentiles together on the cross into one new man. Therefore, Christ's crucifixion was a creating.

E. To Be the One New Man for the Body of Christ

The one new man is for the Body of Christ (Eph. 2:16). To build up the Body, the God-men as the constituents of the new man must be raised up by growing up (Eph. 4:15). The spiritual raising up is not like the natural cultivation. It is to raise up the God-men to grow unto maturity, so that these God-men will do the work of building up the Body of Christ (vv. 12, 16).

F. Having the Believers as His Constituents, Who Are Christ and in Whom Is Christ

The constituents of the new man are the believers, the God-men, who are Christ and in whom is Christ (Col. 3:10-11). According to Colossians 3:11, Christ is all the members of the new man and in all the members. He is everything in the new man. Actually, He is the new man, His Body (1 Cor. 12:12). In the new man He is the centrality and universality. He is the constituent of the new man, and He is all in all in the new man.

G. To Be the Corporate Christ

All the God-men are the corporate Christ. This corporate Christ is in all the constituents, the members, of the new man. This means that the new man, as the totality of the God-men, becomes the corporate Christ. What kind of teaching could cause us to become Christ and even the corporate Christ? Only the teaching of the Bible. The Bible teaches the God-men to constitute the new man, and the new man is the corporate Christ.

H. By the Believers Putting Off the Old Man and Putting On the New Man through the Renewing of the Spirit in Their Mind

The new man was created by Christ, but the believers need to partake of this creation. To bring forth this new man, first Christ's creating work on His cross was needed. Christ has already accomplished that work. In addition, every day we need to put off the old man and put on the new man through the renewing of the spirit in our mind (Eph. 4:22-24).

Our spirit is mingled with the divine Spirit (Rom. 8:16). Today our spirit is not a single spirit; it is a mingled spirit. This mingled spirit can enter into our mind. By our loving the Lord, by our praying to the Lord, and by our reading the Bible, our mind is filled with the mingled spirit. This changes and renews our mind. Our renewed mind then becomes a renewing mind. After I was saved I began to love the Lord, to pray to Him, and to read His Word year after year. This brought the mingled spirit into my mind, and this mingled spirit within me changed my mind, my view, and my thinking. Such a changed mind renews our entire being. This is to complete Christ's creating of the new man.

Christ created the new man, but this creating has not yet been consummated. Christ has created us to be a new man, but after we are saved, we need to partake of this creation by putting off the old man and putting on the new man by having our mind filled with our mingled spirit. All these words are a heavenly language; they have nothing to do with philosophy or human logic. This is the divine revelation from the Bible. We all need to see this. Because I have seen this, no one can change me in my vision.

I. To Be the New Creation of God

The new man, created by Christ on the cross and consummated by our putting off the old man and putting on the new man through the renewing of our mind by the mingled spirit, eventually becomes the new creation of God. The God-men constitute the new man, and the new man eventually becomes the new creation.

1. In Christ as the Element

The new creation is in Christ as the element (2 Cor. 5:17). The very Christ is the element, the factor, of the new creation.

2. As the Unique Accomplishment
in God's Economy

The new creation is the unique accomplishment in God's economy (Gal. 6:15). The consummate point of God's economy is the new creation. This new creation eventually becomes the New Jerusalem as the ultimate consummation of God's divine work (Rev. 21:2) carried out through four ages of humanity by God Himself in Christ and through the Spirit as the Triune God. By God in Christ through the Spirit in our spirit, this new creation is consummated to be the New Jerusalem. This will show God's wisdom, as a shame to God's enemy Satan in his cosmos (Eph. 3:10).

THE INTRINSIC CONTENT
OF THE TEACHING OF THE BIBLE

In this chapter we have covered three main things: the God-men, the new man, and the new creation. The God-men are the believers in Christ, who are reborn of God to be His sons. These sons possess God's divine life and His divine nature. They live by this divine life with this divine nature to constitute the new man.

According to the Bible the new man was created by Christ on the cross and is consummated by the Spirit in our spirit. Christ created the new man in His death. In His death He terminated the old, fallen man and redeemed the original man created by God. At the same time He released the divine life from within Him and imparted this divine life into the redeemed humanity. The new man was created in this way. However, according to the Bible, the new man still must be consummated. The new man is consummated by the Spirit, who is the reality of Christ's resurrection, which is a continuation of His death. Such a Spirit works in the believers to put off the old man, which Christ crucified on the cross, and to put on the new man, which Christ brought forth by imparting Himself as life into the redeemed humanity. The Spirit consummates what Christ created as the new man, in the way of renewing the believers by putting off the old man and putting on the new man through the

renewing of their mind, which is saturated by the Spirit in
their spirit, which becomes the mingled spirit in their mind to
renew their entire person. Today in the universe there is
such a man, on the one hand constituted of the God-men, and
on the other hand created by Christ through His death and
consummated by the Spirit through the renewing within the
believers.

This new man needs to work, to move, and to carry out
something. To do this, the new man needs a new universe.
This new universe is the new creation. The new man is the
person to carry out something in the new creation as the new
universe. In this new universe, which is the new creation, the
new man as a corporate person, the enlarged and corporate
Christ, brings forth the Body of Christ, which is the very good
pleasure and heart's desire of God. This one Body of Christ
consummates the New Jerusalem as God's ultimate goal to
fulfill God's eternal economy.

For the past nineteen centuries thousands of Bible lovers
have studied the Bible. If they were asked what the Bible
teaches, they would give many different answers. What I
have presented to you in this chapter is the highest standard
of what the Bible teaches. The Bible teaches only five things:
the God-men, the new man, the new creation, the Body of
Christ, and the New Jerusalem. The first three—the God-
men, the new man, and the new creation—are the factors to
bring forth one object of two aspects—the Body of Christ and
the New Jerusalem. The God-men, the new man, and the new
creation are for the producing of the Body of Christ, which
will consummate the New Jerusalem as God's ultimate goal.
This is the real and intrinsic understanding of what the Bible
teaches.

In the past seventy-three years, from 1922 until the
present, the Lord in His recovery has used us to develop the
intrinsic understanding of His Word. In these seventy-three
years Brother Watchman Nee's ministry occupied the first
thirty years, from 1922 to 1952, the year he was imprisoned.
During that period Brother Nee laid a very good foundation.
From 1952 until today, a period of forty-three years, we, the
co-workers of Brother Nee, have continued to develop what

he laid as a foundation. In the past two years we have reached the ultimate consummation of our development. This development consummates in the God-men, the new man, the new creation, the Body of Christ, and the New Jerusalem. This is the conclusion of our seventy-three years of labor on this Holy Book. I believe that nothing could be higher than this. In the past two years I have been occupied with this day and night. To release this high revelation, there is a need to put out the crystallization-study of the holy Word.

The intrinsic content of the teaching of the Bible is the God-men, the new man, the new creation, the Body of Christ, and the New Jerusalem. In this chapter we have covered the first three of these items—the God-men, the new man, and the new creation. We need to receive a clear impression that we believers are the God-born God-men to grow in order to constitute the new man. The new man was created by Christ through His death and is consummated by the Spirit through His renewing. This new man becomes a person to move and work out God's purpose in a new universe, that is, the new creation.

CHAPTER TWO

THE GOD-MEN AND THE BODY OF CHRIST

Scripture Reading: Eph. 4:2-6, 11-16

OUTLINE

I. The God-men:
   A. The God-men as the children of God are the members of the Body of Christ—Rom. 12:5.
   B. The God-men as the new man are for the building up of the Body of Christ—Eph. 4:12.
   C. The God-men as the stewards (Luke 12:42; Col. 1:25) struggle for the growth and maturity of the Body of Christ—Col. 1:28-29:
      1. Until it becomes a full-grown man with the measure of the stature of the fullness of Christ—Eph. 4:13.
      2. No longer any of its members remain as little children tossed by waves and carried about by every wind of divisive teaching—Eph. 4:14.
   D. The God-men as the myriads of the multiplied reproduction of the Triune God consummate the Body of Christ as His increase (John 3:30) and fullness (Eph. 1:23) to be the corporate enlargement and fullness as the expression of the processed and consummated Triune God (Eph. 3:19).
II. The Body of Christ:
   A. The church of God (1 Cor. 10:32) as the manifestation of God in the flesh (1 Tim. 3:15-16) is organically the Body of Christ—Eph. 1:22-23.

B. A divine and human constitution constituted with:
   1. The regenerated and transformed believers as its outward, visible frame—its members—Eph. 5:30.
   2. The processed and consummated Triune God as its inward, invisible content:
      a. God the Father, who is over all, through all, and in all, triune in Himself, as the source of all.
      b. God the Son, who is the Lord, as its element.
      c. God the Spirit as its essence—Eph. 4:4-6.
C. A mystical and spiritual Body built up by:
   1. Its particularly gifted members as apostles, prophets, evangelists, and shepherds and teachers, the joints of the rich supply—Eph. 4:11-12, 16.
   2. Its each one part operating according to its measure—Eph. 4:16.
D. The organism of the Triune God consummated by:
   1. The growing in the divine life of all the members of the Body of Christ into Christ, the Head—Eph. 4:15.
   2. Its building up of itself in love—Eph. 4:16.
E. The keeping of the oneness of such a Body—Eph. 4:2-3:
   1. The unique oneness of the Spirit.
   2. Kept diligently:
      a. With all lowliness, meekness, and long-suffering.
      b. Bearing one another in love.
      c. In the uniting bond of peace.

In this chapter we will consider the God-men and the Body of Christ.

I. THE GOD-MEN

A. The God-men as the Children of God Being the Members of the Body of Christ

The God-men as the children of God are the members of the Body of Christ (Rom. 12:5). For the God-men to be the members of the Body of Christ means that they are the constituents of the Body.

B. The God-men as the New Man Being for the Building Up of the Body of Christ

The God-men as the new man are for the building up of the Body of Christ (Eph. 4:12). They are not only the members of the Body of Christ but also the builders of the Body. The Body is built up by its members; that is, it is built up by itself (v. 16).

C. The God-men as the Stewards Struggling for the Growth and Maturity of the Body of Christ

The God-men as the stewards (Luke 12:42; Col. 1:25) struggle for the growth and maturity of the Body of Christ (Col. 1:28-29). It is not sufficient for the God-men to be the builders of the Body. There is the need for some of the God-men to be stewards, like Paul, to struggle and strive for the growth of the Body of Christ. As members of the Body of Christ we need to grow, and as the builders of the Body of Christ we need not only growth but also maturity. It is not adequate merely to grow—we need to mature. For us to grow means not only that the members of the Body of Christ are growing; it also means that the Body itself is growing. The Body needs members; the Body needs the builders; and the Body needs some stewards to promote the growth and maturity of the Body itself.

1. Until the Body of Christ Becomes
a Full-grown Man with the Measure
of the Stature of the Fullness of Christ

These stewards struggle for the growth and maturity of the Body of Christ until the Body becomes a full-grown man, a corporate Christ, with the measure of the stature of the fullness of Christ (Eph. 4:13). Christ has a fullness, the fullness has a stature, and the stature has a measure. The fullness of Christ is the Body of Christ (1:23), which has a stature with a measure. As Christ's fullness the Body is Christ's expression. Christ's fullness, the Body, has a stature, and with this stature there is a certain measure. To arrive at the measure of the stature of the fullness of Christ is to arrive at the full building up of the Body of Christ. It is to arrive at the full completion of the building up of the Body. This is our goal, and we must diligently press toward it until we all reach it together.

2. No Longer Any of Its Members
Remaining as Little Children Tossed
by Waves and Carried About
by Every Wind of Divisive Teaching

The stewards struggle for the growth and maturity of the Body of Christ so that no longer any of its members will remain as little children tossed by waves and carried about by every wind of divisive teaching (4:14). Any teaching, even a scriptural one, that distracts believers from Christ and the church is a wind that carries believers away from God's central purpose. The waves stirred up by the winds of different teachings (1 Tim. 1:3-4), doctrines, concepts, and opinions are sent by Satan to entice the believers in order to carry them away from Christ and the church. It is difficult for infants in Christ to discern these. The only way to escape from the waves that are stirred up by the winds is to grow in life, and the safe way to grow in life is to stay in the proper church life with Christ and the church as the safeguard.

Unfortunately, millions of Christians remain in childhood. They are little children tossed by waves and carried about by every wind of divisive teaching. This is the situation of today's Christianity. On a smaller scale it is also the situation among us, and some, who are still little children, have been carried away into divisions by the winds of dissenting teachings.

D. The God-men as the Myriads of the Multiplied Reproduction of the Triune God Consummating the Body of Christ as His Increase and Fullness

The God-men as the myriads of the multiplied reproduction of the Triune God consummate the Body of Christ as His increase (John 3:30) and fullness (Eph. 1:23) to be the corporate enlargement and fullness as the expression of the processed and consummated Triune God (3:19). In relation to the Body of Christ, the God-men are not only the members, the builders, and the stewards but are also the reproduction of the Triune God. As such, they consummate the Body of Christ as His increase and fullness. Eventually, this increase and fullness will become enlarged and will become the enlargement of the processed and consummated Triune God for His eternal expression.

II. THE BODY OF CHRIST

A. The Church of God as the Manifestation of God in the Flesh

The church of God (1 Cor. 10:32) as the manifestation of God in the flesh (1 Tim. 3:15-16) is organically the Body of Christ (Eph. 1:22-23). The church of the living God is the house of God, which is the manifestation of God in the flesh. The living God, who lives in the church, is subjective to the church. Because He is living, the church too is living in Him, by Him, and with Him. A living God and a living church live, move, and work together. The living church is the house and household of the living God. Hence, it becomes the manifestation of God in the flesh.

In 1 Timothy 3:16 Paul says, "Great is the mystery of godliness: He who was manifested in the flesh..." The mystery of godliness is God becoming man that man may become God in life and in nature but not in the Godhead. This mystery of godliness is the manifestation of God in the flesh. The word *He* refers to Christ, who was God manifested in the flesh. As the organic Body of Christ, the church of God is the continuation of Christ as the manifestation of God in the flesh.

B. A Divine and Human Constitution

The Body of Christ is a divine and human constitution.

1. Constituted with the Regenerated and Transformed Believers as Its Outward, Visible Frame

The Body of Christ is constituted with the regenerated and transformed believers as its outward, visible frame—its members (Eph. 5:30).

2. Constituted with the Processed and Consummated Triune God as Its Inward, Invisible Content

As a divine and human constitution, the Body of Christ is also constituted with the processed and consummated Triune God as its inward, invisible content (4:4-6). Whereas the frame is outward and visible, the content is inward and invisible. The outward, visible frame is the believers, and the inward, invisible content is the Triune God.

a. God the Father as the Source of All

God the Father, who is over all, through all, and in all, triune in Himself, is the source of all. As the source of the Body of Christ, God the Father is the Originator, the Initiator.

b. God the Son as Its Element

God the Son, who is the Lord, is the element of the Body of Christ. Every substance has its element, its nature. Christ is the element for the constituting of the Body of Christ; He is the element with which the Body of Christ is constituted.

c. God the Spirit as Its Essence

God the Spirit is the essence of the Body. The essence of a certain thing is within the element of that thing. To get the essence it is necessary to extract the essence from the element. Let us use an orange as an illustration. The element of an orange is simply the orange itself. The essence of the orange is the juice. If you extract the juice from the orange, then you will have the essence of the element of the orange. From this illustration we can see the difference between element and essence. Regarding the Body of Christ the Son is the element, and the Spirit is the essence of the element for the constituting of the Body of Christ as a divine and human constitution.

Have you seen what the Body of Christ is? The Body of Christ is a constitution, constituted with the believers as the outward frame and with the Triune God as the inward content. This content has a source, an element, and an essence. The source is God the Father, the element is God the Son, and the essence is God the Spirit.

Whereas many of the teachings in Christianity are the "orange peel," the teaching in the Lord's recovery concerning the Body of Christ is a teaching of the element with the essence. For many of today's Christians the Body of Christ is merely a term, but, by the Lord's mercy, we have seen that the Body of Christ is a divine and human constitution constituted with the regenerated and transformed believers and the processed and consummated Triune God.

C. A Mystical and Spiritual Body

The Body of Christ is also a mystical and spiritual Body.

1. Built Up by Its Particularly Gifted Members

This mystical and spiritual Body is built up by its particularly gifted members as apostles, prophets, evangelists, and shepherds and teachers, the joints of the rich supply (Eph. 4:11-12, 16). They are builders of the Body.

Those who are the particularly gifted members of the Body should not regard themselves as different from all the other members. For example, in our physical body the nose and the eyes are particularly gifted members, but they are still members of the body, not something else. The principle is the same with the members of the Body of Christ. The particularly gifted members are still nothing more than members of the Body. However, many of today's ministers and pastors do not regard themselves as members but as "lords." By the Lord's grace I can testify that no matter how much I speak for God, I always consider myself a brother in the Lord and a member of the Body. I do not want others to give me any kind of title, for I am just a member and a brother.

2. Built Up by Its Each One Part

The mystical and spiritual Body is built up also by its each one part operating according to its measure (v. 16). Instead of being a particularly gifted member of the Body, you may be a common, general member. It is wonderful to be such a member. The common members are also the builders of the Body. As a common member of the Body, you should function according to your measure. By these two kinds of members, the particularly gifted members as the joints of the rich supply and the common members with their measure, the Body is built up.

D. The Organism of the Triune God

The Body of Christ is also the organism of the Triune God. An illustration of this organism is found in John 15—the vine with all its branches. The vine is developed and enlarged through its branches. This organism grows with the riches of the Triune God and expresses the divine life. This is a picture of the Body of Christ as the organism of the Triune God.

1. Consummated by the Growing in the Divine Life of All the Members into the Head

As the organism of the Triune God, the Body of Christ is consummated by the growing in the divine life of all the members of the Body into Christ, the Head (Eph. 4:15). Paul speaks of growing up into the Head, Christ, in all things. To grow in this way is to have Christ increase in us in all things until we attain to a full-grown man. The word *Head* in verse 15 indicates that our growth in life by the increase of Christ should be the growth of the members of the Body under the Head. We all need to grow into the Head, Christ, so that the Body of Christ as the organism of the Triune God may be consummated.

2. Consummated by Its Building Up of Itself in Love

The organism of the Triune God is consummated also by its building up of itself in love (v. 16). Love is the inner substance of God. Thus, the love in which the Body of Christ builds itself up is not our own love but the love of God in Christ, which becomes the love of Christ in us. By this love we love Christ and the fellow members of His Body.

The building up of the Body of Christ is consummated by our growing into Christ and by the Body building up itself in love. This indicates that our growing into Christ is a kind of self-building, for our growing into Christ is part of the building up of the Body. Therefore, the Body is built up consummately by the growing of all the members into Christ. This is the Body building up itself in love.

E. The Keeping of the Oneness of the Body

We need to keep the oneness of the Body of Christ (vv. 2-3).

1. The Unique Oneness of the Spirit

The oneness of the Body of Christ is the unique oneness of the Spirit. This oneness is in all of us. We all have the oneness which is the Spirit who is the essence of the Body. The Spirit is both the essence of the Body and the oneness of the Body. This means that the essence of the Body is the oneness of the Body.

Those who are divisive know essentially that they are divisive. They will not admit this or confess it, but deep within them there is an essential factor which tells them that they are divisive. On the contrary, we may have the full assurance that we are not divisive but are keeping the unique oneness of the Spirit. There is an essential factor within us which testifies that we are keeping the oneness of the Body. Regarding the unique oneness of the Spirit as the oneness of the Body, there is an essential judgment within the believers.

2. Kept Diligently

The oneness of the Body must be kept diligently. According to Paul's word in Ephesians 4:2-3 we keep the oneness of the Spirit with all lowliness, meekness, and long-suffering and by bearing one another in love. Furthermore, we keep the unique oneness of the Body of Christ in the uniting bond of peace.

CHAPTER THREE

THE GOD-MEN AND THE OVERCOMERS

Scripture Reading: Rev. 2:7, 11, 17, 26; 3:5, 12, 21

OUTLINE

I. The God-men:
   A. Born of God to overcome sin and the world—
      1 John 3:9; 5:4.
   B. Destined by God to conquer all the oppositions
      and persecutions, the hard environments, and the
      difficult situations—Rom. 8:31, 36-39.
   C. Called by the Lord among the churches to be the
      overcomers—Rev. 2:7, 11, 17, 26; 3:5, 12, 21.
II. The overcomers:
   A. To overcome in the degradation of the churches:
      1. The satanic Judaism—Rev. 2:9-10.
      2. The demonic Catholicism—2:24-28.
      3. The dead and Christless Protestantism—3:1-5,
         20-21.
      4. The tide of the church's degradation.
   B. To overcome also:
      1. Satan—12:11a.
      2. The love of the soul-life—12:11b.
      3. The upcoming Antichrist and his false prophet
         in the great tribulation—15:2; 17:14.
III. The way for the God-men to be the overcomers:
   A. To love Christ and follow Him—John 21:15-17, 19b.
   B. To pursue Christ and gain Him—Phil. 3:12-15.
   C. To be conformed to the death of Christ by the
      power of His resurrection—Phil. 3:10.
   D. To live Christ and magnify Him by the bountiful
      supply of His all-inclusive Spirit—Phil. 1:19-21.

    E. To live with Christ and labor with Him—Gal.
2:20a; Col. 1:29.

    F. To live the Body life and build up the Body of
Christ for the fulfillment of God's New Testament
economy—Eph. 4:12, 16; 1:10.

IV. The reward for the overcoming God-men, the overcomers, in the millennial kingdom:

    A. In the present age—to dine with the Lord—Rev.
3:20b.

    B. At the earliest appearing of Christ—to be given
the morning star, signifying the precious Christ in
His earliest appearing—Rev. 2:28.

    C. In the millennial kingdom:

        1. To enter richly into the kingdom of Christ—
2 Pet. 1:11; Matt. 19:23; Acts 14:22; 2 Thes. 1:5;
Heb. 12:28; James 2:5; cf. 1 Cor. 6:9; Gal. 5:21;
Eph. 5:5.

        2. To partake of the wedding feast of Christ,
which will last for one thousand years as a
day—Rev. 19:9; Matt. 25:10.

        3. To have their names confessed before the
Father and His angels by the Lord—Rev. 3:5c.

        4. Not to have their names erased out of the book
of life, to have their names erased out of the
book of life in the kingdom age signifying a
kind of discipline in the kingdom age—Rev.
3:5b.

        5. Not to be hurt of the second death, to be hurt of
the second death probably signifying also a
kind of discipline in the kingdom age—Rev.
2:11.

        6. To participate in the consummation and enjoy-
ment of the New Jerusalem as the Paradise of
God in its initial stage in the millennium—Rev.
2:7.

        7. To share in the joy of the Lord—Matt. 25:21, 23.

        8. To be crowned with the crown, the crown of life
and the crown of righteousness—Rev. 3:11;
1 Cor. 9:25; Rev. 2:10; James 1:12; 2 Tim. 4:8.

9. To sit with the Lord on His throne—Rev. 3:21.
10. To have authority over the nations—Rev. 2:26-27.
11. To be priests of God and of Christ and reign with Christ in the millennial kingdom—Rev. 20:4-6; 2 Tim. 2:12.
12. To eat of the tree of life in the New Jerusalem in its initial stage in the millennial kingdom—Rev. 2:7.
13. To eat the hidden manna—Rev. 2:17a.
14. To be clothed with white garments—Rev. 3:4-5a.
15. To be a pillar in the temple of God and never to go out anymore—Rev. 3:12a.
16. To be given a white stone with a new name written upon it—Rev. 2:17b.
17. To have the name of God and the name of the city of God—the New Jerusalem—and the Lord's new name written upon them—Rev. 3:12b.
18. To be given the responsibilities in the coming kingdom—Matt. 24:47; 25:21a, 23a.
19. To enjoy the kingdom rest—Heb. 4:1, 9-11.
20. To enjoy the salvation of the soul, which is the aggregate of the above nineteen points—Matt. 16:25; Luke 9:24; Heb. 10:39; 1 Pet. 1:9-10.

V. The blessing of God's complete salvation, that is, the enjoyment of the eternal life (Matt. 19:29; Rom. 5:21) for all the God-men in the new heaven and new earth:

A. To participate in the holy city—the New Jerusalem—in its consummated stage as their temple—the Triune God Himself—for their dwelling in eternity—Rev. 22:14b; 21:22.

B. To eat the tree of life—Rev. 22:14a, 2.

C. To enjoy the spring of life and drink the water of life in the river of life—Rev. 21:6; 22:1.

D. To have God as their God and to be sons of God—Rev. 21:7.

E. To participate in the divine and human marriage life of the processed and consummated Triune God and the transformed and glorified tripartite man—Rev. 21:9.

F. To serve God as priests and to reign as kings over the nations forever and ever—Rev. 22:3b, 5b.

G. To have no curse and no night but to enjoy God's shining as their light—Rev. 22:3, 5; 21:25, 23.

VI. The destiny of all "Christians":

A. The Catholic Church as the great Babylon will be burned—Rev. 17:5, 16.

B. The false Christians, the tares, in all kinds of churches will be bound into bundles to be burned up in the lake of fire—Matt. 13:30, 40-42.

C. The genuine but defeated believers:

1. Their work and conduct as wood, grass, and stubble will be burned at the Lord's coming.

2. They themselves will be saved, yet so as through fire—1 Cor. 3:12-15.

3. They will be disciplined (Matt. 25:30) and transformed to be mature and perfect so that they will be qualified to participate in the New Jerusalem in its consummated stage for eternity.

D. The genuine and overcoming believers, the overcomers, whose work and conduct are like gold, silver, and precious stones:

1. They will be rewarded (1 Cor. 3:12-15; Rom. 14:10; 2 Cor. 5:10; 1 Cor. 4:5; Matt. 25:19) to enter into the coming millennial kingdom to reign with the Lord and partake of His joy, as revealed in the above list of their rewards.

2. They will be joined by the God-men perfected in the millennial kingdom in the participation of the final consummation and enjoyment of the New Jerusalem in its consummated stage for eternity.

In this chapter we will consider the God-men and the overcomers.

I. THE GOD-MEN

A. Born of God to Overcome Sin and the World

The God-men are born of God to overcome sin and the world (1 John 3:9; 5:4). As God-men, we were born not only to be saved but also to overcome. First John 3:9 tells us that we were born to overcome sin. Then 5:4 tells us that we were born to overcome the world. Sin and the world are two big seducers. Within us sin is seducing us continually, and outside us the world seduces us. To be an overcomer, we need to overcome the first line of the enemy. In a battle there are battle lines. We have been born of God to overcome the first line of the enemy, which consists of two items, sin and the world.

B. Destined by God to Conquer
All the Oppositions and Persecutions, the Hard
Environments, and the Difficult Situations

Not only so, we are destined by God to conquer all the oppositions and persecutions, the hard environments, and the difficult situations (Rom. 8:31, 36-39). After being saved, we, the God-men, are destined to travel not on a plain, smooth highway but on a rugged way full of troubles, trials, temptations, persecutions, attacks, and oppositions (John 15:20a; Acts 14:22; 1 Thes. 3:4; 2 Tim. 3:12; 2 Cor. 11:23-27). Before we were saved, many of us had a smooth family life. Because we believed in the Lord Jesus, our family life may have become very rugged. Nevertheless, we are destined to conquer. This is the second line of the enemy that we must overcome.

After being saved, many Christians are unable to overcome sin and the world. Rather, they become indulgent in their lust and in their enjoyment of worldly pleasures. Some believers temporarily overcome sin and the world, but they are not able to overcome the problems and the difficulties and all kinds of attacks, criticisms, persecutions, and oppositions. They do not dare to take the Lord's way, which is a constricted and rugged way (Matt. 7:14). Hence, they compromise with the opposition that they encounter. For example, to please his unsaved wife, a believing husband may compromise by participating with her in the enjoyment of worldly entertainments and pleasures. Many Christians know that they should overcome certain things, but when they are threatened by opposition, they compromise.

Concerning the church life, some Christian leaders know that the denominations are wrong, but they dare not say anything. They dare not give up their involvement with their denomination, because they are afraid of losing their position as a pastor or a minister. This is the second line of the enemy that we must overcome.

C. Called by the Lord among the Churches to Be the Overcomers

Sin and the world are the first line of Satan, and the oppositions and persecutions, hard environments, and difficult situations are the second line. In addition to these two lines, the enemy has built up a third line to frustrate the lovers of Christ from going on to follow Him. This third line is the degradation of the churches. The God-men are born of God to overcome the first line of Satan, and they are destined by God to conquer the second line. To overcome the third line, the God-men have been called by the Lord among the churches to be the overcomers (Rev. 2:7, 11, 17, 26; 3:5, 12, 21).

II. THE OVERCOMERS

A. To Overcome in the Degradation of the Churches

As we have pointed out, the third line of the enemy is the degradation of the churches. The churches themselves are not the enemies, but the degradation, the degraded situation, the degraded condition, of the churches has become a real enemy to us. In overcoming the degradation of the churches, we need to overcome three "isms"—satanic Judaism (Rev. 2:9-10), demonic Catholicism (2:24-28), and dead and Christless Protestantism (3:1-5, 20-21).

1. The Satanic Judaism

In Revelation 2:9 the Lord Jesus called the Jewish syna-gogue "a synagogue of Satan" (see note 9[5]—New Testament Recovery Version). Today people consider Judaism a typical religion, but they do not know that in the eyes of God Juda-ism has become satanic. This is not my word but the word of the Lord Jesus in Revelation 2:9.

Today in the New Testament age of grace one of the strongest oppositions to God's economy is Judaism. In the past nineteen centuries millions of Gentiles have turned to Christ, but from the time of the destruction of Jerusalem in A.D. 70 until today, comparatively few Jews have turned to the Lord. In preaching the gospel to sinners, it is much more diffi-cult to win a Jew to Christ than to gain a Gentile for the Lord. Hence, today the Jewish religion is a strong enemy against Jesus Christ. For this reason the Jewish believers need to hear the Lord's voice and overcome the synagogue of Satan. Otherwise, they cannot be lovers, followers, and pursuers of Christ. Rather, they will be defeated in God's eyes.

2. The Demonic Catholicism

The phrase *demonic Catholicism* refers to the Roman Catholic Church. I say that the Catholic Church is demonic, because in Revelation 2:24 the Lord Jesus, speaking to the church in Thyatira, a prefigure of the apostate Roman Catholic Church, said that in her there were "the deep things of Satan." Because the Catholic Church teaches the deep things of the philosophy of the satanic mysteries (cf. 1 Tim. 4:1-3), it has become demonic, related to the demons.

In Revelation 2:20 the Lord Jesus referred to the woman Jezebel, a figure signifying the apostate Roman Church. The woman Jezebel is the same woman as the one mentioned by the Lord Jesus in Matthew 13:33. There the woman added leaven (signifying evil, heretical, and pagan things—1 Cor. 5:6, 8; Matt. 16:6, 11-12) into the fine flour. The fine flour refers to the teachings concerning Christ. All the teachings concern-ing Christ should be very nourishing, like the flour of wheat. But the woman mixed many evil, heretical, and pagan things into the teachings concerning Christ. The Catholic Church has fully leavened in a hidden way all the teachings concerning Christ. This is the actual situation in the Roman Catholic Church. Eventually, the Catholic Church, signified by the woman in Matthew 13:33 and by Jezebel, the pagan wife of Ahab, becomes the great harlot, Babylon the Great, in Revelation 17.

On the one hand, the Catholic Church teaches that Jesus Christ is the Son of God. On the other hand, they teach the worship of Mary, the "holy mother." This is a great heresy added into the truth concerning Christ. Today's Christmas is another example of leaven added by Catholicism to the fine flour of the teaching concerning Christ. In ancient times December 25 was the day on which the Romans worshipped their sun god. Later, after many Romans became false Christians under the seducing of Constantine the Great, they still wanted to continue their remembrance of the sun god. However, under the influence of Constantine, they were forced to worship Christ. Therefore, they made December 25 a day for the celebration of Christ's birth. This is the source of Christmas. Christ is true; Christmas is false. Christ is the truth; Christmas is a heresy and a mixture. Over the centuries some books have been written, including *The Two Babylons* by Alexander Hislop, to expose the heresies of Roman Catholicism.

What I have told you is the truth concerning the Roman Catholic Church. In the Lord's recovery we do not teach anything out of the depths of Satan. We teach everything based on the strong word in the Bible. Although we may be attacked by those who are sympathetic toward Catholicism, no one can defeat us, because we have the truth, and the truth will prevail.

3. The Dead and Christless Protestantism

In Revelation 3:1-2, speaking to the church in Sardis, a prefigure of the Protestant churches from the time of the Reformation, the Lord Jesus said, "I know your works, that you have a name that you are living, and yet you are dead. Become watchful and establish the things which remain, which were about to die; for I have found none of your works completed before My God." Here the Lord Jesus tells us that the Protestant churches are dead and that the things that remain in them are about to die. Today everything in Protestant Christianity is dead or is dying. This is not my word but the word of the Lord Jesus. Then, in Revelation 3:20 the Lord Jesus was knocking on the door of the church in Laodicea, indicating that He was outside the church in Laodicea. Thus, the church in Laodicea, a prefigure of the degraded Brethren assemblies as part of today's Protestantism, is Christless. This is the actual situation of today's Christianity. On the one hand, the Protestant churches are dead or are dying in spiritual things. On the other hand, they claim to preach Christ, but they do not have Christ actually living within them. In this sense they are Christless.

4. The Tide of the Church's Degradation

The degradation of the church today has become a tide that we, the God-men, must overcome. In the entire Christianity there is a trend of decline, a tide of degradation. According to my observation, over the past thirty years Christianity has been continually going downhill. The most sinful things have been brought into today's Christianity. Today, because of the degraded situation, many people will not go to certain churches. In many denominations the number of Sunday-goers is decreasing. This is a sign of the tide of the church's degradation.

B. To Overcome Also:

1. Satan

The God-men also need to overcome Satan, the accuser of the brothers (Rev. 12:11a).

2. The Love of the Soul-life

In Revelation 2:10b the persecuted saints in the church in Smyrna were charged by the Lord to be faithful unto death. In 12:11b the overcomers overcome Satan, the accuser, by three things: by the blood of the Lamb, by the word of their testimony, and by not loving their soul-life even unto death. We need to overcome the love of the soul-life by sacrificing all the enjoyments, pleasures, and entertainments of the soul. Some of the saints may desire to drive an expensive car, to wear costly clothing, and to live in a magnificent house. This is the enjoyment of the soul in living luxuriously.

The reason we are not willing to go out to knock on doors to save sinners to make them members of Christ may be because we like to rest and do not like to lose our face in being rejected by people. This is the loving of the soul-life.

Very few are willing to pay the price at the cost of sacrificing themselves to take this way. This is why the Lord called this way the narrow way, in contrast to the broad way (Matt. 7:13-14). To overcome the love of the soul-life, the Lord will lead you to have many changes. He will lead you to give up the enjoyments of the soul.

3. The Upcoming Antichrist and His False Prophet in the Great Tribulation

At the end of this age there will be a time of great tribulation (Matt. 24:21). During this time Antichrist will rise up (Rev. 13:1), and his false prophet also will rise up (v. 11). They will persecute all the children of God (vv. 7, 15). The overcomers must overcome that persecution (15:2; 17:14).

III. THE WAY FOR THE GOD-MEN TO BE THE OVERCOMERS

The way for the God-men to be the overcomers is first to love Christ and follow Him (John 21:15-17, 19b). The God-men as the overcomers must also pursue Christ and gain Him (Phil. 3:12-15), and they must be conformed to the death of Christ by the power of His resurrection (v. 10). In everything we need to be conformed to Christ's death. In everything we should be crucified. It should be "no longer I," because the "I" has been crossed out (Gal. 2:20a). In ourselves it is impossible for us to be conformed to Christ's death. However, we do have the resurrected Christ living within us. We should rely on the power of His resurrection that we may be conformed to His death in everything. Many times I realized that I was not conformed to the Lord's death in my attitude toward my wife. After speaking just one short sentence in an unpleasant tone, I realized that I was not conformed to the death of Christ. I have repented for such sins nearly every day for many years.

The overcomers also need to live Christ and magnify Him by the bountiful supply of His all-inclusive Spirit (Phil. 1:19-21). Today the Spirit is not only the Spirit of God but also the Spirit of Jesus Christ, who has the bountiful supply for us to live Christ and magnify Christ.

In order to overcome, the God-men also need to live with Christ and labor with Him (Gal. 2:20a; Col. 1:29). Finally, they should not live merely an individual Christian life but must live the Body life, a corporate life, and build up the Body of Christ for the fulfillment of God's New Testament economy (Eph. 4:12, 16; 1:10).

IV. THE REWARD FOR THE OVERCOMING GOD-MEN, THE OVERCOMERS, IN THE MILLENNIAL KINGDOM

God has prepared all kinds of blessings in the New Jerusalem. Every part, every aspect, and every item of the New Jerusalem is a blessing prepared by God for His chosen and saved ones. However, God realizes that many of His chosen and saved ones would not be faithful to Him. Hence, He has established the principle of the overcomers. God the Lord came in to call the saved ones to overcome all the things that oppose God. Most of the God-called and saved believers would not listen to this call. Therefore, in the millennium the overcoming believers will be rewarded by participating in the enjoyment of the kingdom, but all the defeated ones will miss the reward. Furthermore, because they are not mature in life, God will have to perfect them by disciplining and punishing them during the thousand years. The overcomers will enjoy the blessing of God's complete salvation one thousand years earlier as a reward. Those who do not overcome will miss the one-thousand-year enjoyment of the blessing of God's salvation, and they will also be punished by the Lord during that period so that they can be perfected and matured.

Some dear saints do not like to be a Christian who takes such a narrow way. They may not like it today, but sooner or later the Lord will force them to like it. We have been chosen by Him (Eph. 1:4; 1 Pet. 1:2); it is not up to us. We must overcome. If we do not overcome today, we will have to overcome tomorrow. In a school all the students must graduate. If they do not study well, they will not graduate with the rest of their class. Nevertheless, eventually they still need to graduate. Therefore, they have to remain in school for another period of time and must be forced to study until they graduate.

In the thousand years of the millennium the items of the eternal blessing of God's complete salvation will become a reward to the overcomers. In the present age the overcomers dine with the Lord, that is, feast with the Lord, as a reward (Rev. 3:20b). At the earliest appearing of Christ, the overcomers will be given the morning star, signifying the precious Christ in His earliest appearing (2:28).

In the millennial kingdom the overcomers will enter richly into the kingdom of Christ (2 Pet. 1:11; Matt. 19:23; Acts 14:22; 2 Thes. 1:5; Heb. 12:28; James 2:5; cf. 1 Cor. 6:9; Gal. 5:21; Eph. 5:5) and will partake of the wedding feast of Christ, which will last for one thousand years as a day (Rev. 19:9; Matt. 25:10). They will also have their names confessed before the Father and His angels by the Lord (Rev. 3:5c) and will not have their names erased out of the book of life, to have their names erased out of the book of life in the kingdom age signifying a kind of discipline in the kingdom age (v. 5b). They will not be hurt of the second death, to be hurt of the second death probably signifying also a kind of discipline in the kingdom age (2:11).

In the age of the kingdom the overcoming God-men will be rewarded with the participation in the consummation and enjoyment of the New Jerusalem as the Paradise of God in its initial stage in the millennium (2:7). The New Jerusalem will have two stages: the initial stage of one thousand years as a reward to the overcomers, and the consummated stage in the new heaven and new earth for eternity for all the completed, perfected, and matured believers.

In the millennium the overcomers will share in the joy of
the Lord (Matt. 25:21, 23) and will also be crowned with the
crown, the crown of life and the crown of righteousness (Rev.
3:11; 1 Cor. 9:25; Rev. 2:10; James 1:12; 2 Tim. 4:8). They will
also sit with the Lord on His throne (Rev. 3:21) and will have
authority over the nations (2:26-27). Moreover, they will be
priests of God and of Christ and reign with Christ (20:4-6;
2 Tim. 2:12) and will eat of the tree of life in the New Jerusalem in its initial stage in the millennial kingdom (Rev. 2:7).
The overcomers will also eat the hidden manna (2:17a) and be
clothed with white garments (3:4-5a). They will be pillars in
the temple of God and never go out anymore (3:12a) and will
also be given a white stone with a new name written upon it
(2:17b). The overcoming God-men will have the name of God
and the name of the city of God—the New Jerusalem—and
the Lord's new name written upon them (3:12b). They will be
given the responsibilities in the coming kingdom (Matt. 24:47;
25:21a, 23a) and will also enjoy the kingdom rest (Heb. 4:1,
9-11).

In the millennial kingdom the overcomers will enjoy the
salvation of the soul, which is the aggregate of all the
above-mentioned items (Matt. 16:25; Luke 9:24; Heb. 10:39;
1 Pet. 1:9-10). This salvation will be the common portion of all
the saints, not in the thousand-year kingdom but in the New
Jerusalem in the new heaven and new earth.

V. THE BLESSING OF GOD'S COMPLETE SALVATION, THAT IS, THE ENJOYMENT OF THE ETERNAL LIFE FOR ALL THE GOD-MEN IN THE NEW HEAVEN AND NEW EARTH

After being perfected and matured, the defeated believers
will join with the overcoming God-men to enjoy the eternal
blessing of God's complete salvation in the new heaven and
new earth (Matt. 19:29; Rom. 5:21). That blessing is just the
New Jerusalem.

In the enjoyment of God's complete salvation, the God-men
will participate in the holy city—the New Jerusalem—in its
consummated stage as their temple—the Triune God Himself—
for their dwelling in eternity (Rev. 22:14b; 21:22). They will

eat the tree of life (22:14a, 2) and enjoy the spring of life and drink the water of life in the river of life (21:6; 22:1).

In the new heaven and new earth the God-men will have God as their God and be sons of God (21:7). They will also participate in the divine and human marriage life of the processed and consummated Triune God and the transformed and glorified tripartite man (v. 9). This is not the wedding, which will be a reward to the overcomers in the millennium; this is the marriage life of the believers with the Triune God for eternity.

In the New Jerusalem all the God-men will serve God as priests and reign as kings over the nations forever and ever (22:3b, 5b). They will have no curse and no night but will enjoy God's shining as their light (vv. 3, 5; 21:25, 23).

VI. THE DESTINY OF ALL "CHRISTIANS"

There are mainly four kinds of "Christians" on the earth today. Some who call themselves Christians are actually not genuine believers but are false, or nominal, Christians. Each kind of "Christian" has a particular destiny.

A. The Catholic Church as the Great Babylon

The first category of "Christians" is the Roman Catholic Church. The Catholic Church as the great Babylon will be burned. This is not my word but the word of the Bible in Revelation 17:5 and 16. There we are told that one day, probably at the beginning of the great tribulation, three and a half years before the one-thousand-year kingdom, God will use Antichrist with his ten kings to execute His judgment on the Catholic Church by burning her utterly with fire.

B. The False Christians, the Tares

The second category of "Christians" is the false Christians, the nominal Christians, who are the tares prophesied by the Lord in Matthew 13:38-42. In a number of so-called churches today there are many false Christians, those who claim to be saved but have never been regenerated by the Spirit. A real Christian is one who not only repents unto God but also receives God in Christ into his being by exercising his spirit to receive Christ into his spirit. By so doing his spirit has a direct contact with Christ as the divine Spirit. This is needed in order for a person to be genuinely saved. Electricity may be installed in a certain building, with all the electrical wires and switches built in. However, the lights in the building will not shine if a connection is not made at the switch so that the electrical current can flow. Once the connection is made, the electrical power operates and the lights shine. A nominal Christian may agree with all the doctrines concerning Christ and may even repent, yet he has never opened himself in his spirit to receive Christ as the Spirit into his spirit. He has never experienced a spiritual "connection" so that the Spirit as the divine electricity can flow into him.

I was born into Christianity and was educated in Christianity. I heard many doctrines, and I proclaimed to others that I was a Christian. When people opposed Christianity, I contradicted them. But I was not saved until I heard the gospel one afternoon in April 1925 at the age of nineteen. At that time I had a direct contact with God. Unless a person has such a contact with God by his spirit contacting God's Spirit, he can never be saved.

The false Christians, the tares, in all kinds of churches will be bound into bundles to be burned up in the lake of fire (Matt. 13:30, 40-42). When the Lord comes back, the first thing He will do in executing His judgment is to send His angels to bind up the false Christians into bundles and cast them directly into the lake of fire. They will not need to pass through the judgment at the white throne mentioned in Revelation 20:11-15. It is terrible to be a false Christian. When the Lord comes back, the false Christians will be the first to be judged. They will be judged at the time of the Lord's coming, one thousand years before the rest of the unbelievers are judged.

C. The Genuine but Defeated Believers

The third category of Christians is the genuine but defeated believers. In 1 Corinthians 3:12 their work and conduct are likened to wood, grass, and stubble, which are good only to be burned. Many genuine Christians are not overcoming but are defeated. At His coming back, the Lord will burn their work and conduct by fire, but the defeated believers themselves will be saved, yet so as through fire (v. 15). Furthermore, they will be disciplined (Matt. 25:30) and transformed to be mature and perfect so that they will be qualified to participate in the New Jerusalem in its consummated stage for eternity. They will have no share in the New Jerusalem in the thousand-year kingdom, but after they are perfected and matured, they will join the New Jerusalem in the new heaven and new earth after the one-thousand-year kingdom.

D. The Genuine and Overcoming Believers, the Overcomers

The fourth category of Christians is the genuine and overcoming believers, the overcomers. In 1 Corinthians 3:12 their work and conduct are likened to gold, silver, and precious stones, which can never be burned. For such a work and conduct they will be rewarded (1 Cor. 3:14; Rom. 14:10; 2 Cor. 5:10; 1 Cor. 4:5; Matt. 25:19) to enter into the coming millennial kingdom to reign with the Lord and partake of His joy, as revealed in the above list of their rewards. They will also enjoy the New Jerusalem as their blessing from the Lord as a reward in the thousand years. After the thousand years they will be joined by the God-men perfected in the millennial kingdom in the participation of the final consummation and enjoyment of the New Jerusalem in its consummated stage for eternity.

We need to be not only genuine Christians but also overcoming Christians. I hope that we will all be the overcomers.

CHAPTER FOUR

THE GOD-MEN AND THE NEW JERUSALEM

(1)

Scripture Reading: Rev. 21—22

OUTLINE

I. The God-men:
   A. The God-men constitute the new man to be the constituents of the New Jerusalem.
   B. The God-men build up the Body of Christ for the building of the New Jerusalem.
   C. The God-men become the overcomers to consummate the New Jerusalem.

II. The New Jerusalem:
   A. The union and mingling of all God's redeemed through all the four ages of the forefathers, the law, grace, and the kingdom with the processed and consummated Triune God.
   B. The consummation of God's new creation out of His old creation in the four ages from the creation of man to the end of time.
   C. An organic constitution constituted with the redeeming processed and consummated Triune God and the redeemed, transformed, and glorified tripartite men as an organism of the consummated Triune God for His eternal enlargement and expression through the glorified tripartite men.
   D. The dwelling place of the processed and consummated Triune God, signified by the tabernacle—Rev. 21:3; cf. John 1:14.
   E. The counterpart of Christ as the embodiment of

the Triune God, indicated by the bride in Christ's
one-thousand-year wedding day and the wife in
eternity, the precursor of which is the church as
the Body of Christ—Rev. 21:2, 9; 19:7, 9; Eph.
5:25-32.

F. The ultimate consummation of the universal woman
in Revelation 12:1.

G. The spreading of the processed and consummated
Triune God through His redeemed, transformed,
and glorified people as His increase for His eternal purpose.

H. The reflection and fulfillment of the divine revelation concerning the garden of Eden:

1. The divine revelation concerning the garden of
Eden, created by the eternal Triune God, and the
divine revelation concerning the New Jerusalem,
builded by the processed and consummated
Triune God, reflecting each other:

a. The revelation concerning the garden of
Eden, as the beginning of the divine revelation in the Holy Scripture, contains—Gen.
2:8-14, 18-24:

1) The tree of life as the center of God's
eternal economy—v. 9a.

2) A river flowing into four heads to reach
the four directions of the earth—vv. 10-14.

3) At the flow of the river three kinds of
precious materials: gold, pearl, and onyx,
scattered and not yet builded together—
vv. 11-12.

4) A couple, signifying Christ and the
church—vv. 18-24; Eph. 5:22-29:

a) The wife came out of the husband
(signifying Christ) as a part (a rib,
signifying the resurrection life of
Christ) of him taken out of him in
his sleep (signifying the death of
Christ) by God, which part God built

into a woman (signifying the church)—
Gen. 2:21-22a.

b) God brought the woman to the man
and made her one flesh with him as
her husband to be his counterpart as
his increase and expression—vv. 22b-
24; John 3:29a, 30; Eph. 1:23.

b. The revelation concerning the New Jerusalem, as the ending of the divine revelation
in the Holy Scripture, contains—Rev. 21:1—
22:2:

1) The tree of life as the center of God's
eternal economy—22:2.

2) A river of water of life flowing to reach
the four directions of the earth—22:1;
cf. 21:13.

3) Three kinds of precious materials: gold,
pearls, and precious stones, built together into a city, the city of New
Jerusalem, by the processed and consummated Triune God—21:18-21.

4) The entire city of New Jerusalem being a
couple:

a) The processed and consummated redeeming Triune God in Christ is the
Husband.

b) The chosen and redeemed people of
the redeeming Triune God are the wife,
produced by the processed and consummated Triune God through Christ's
death and resurrection with the divine
life of the redeeming God as the element to be His counterpart as His
enlargement and expression in eternity—21:2, 9; Eph. 1:23; 3:19.

2. What is revealed in these two parts of the
divine revelation in the Holy Scripture is the
central line of the entire divine revelation
throughout the entire Holy Scripture. This

central line should be a controlling principle to
our interpreting and understanding of the Holy
Scripture.

I. The unique, divine, and organic building in the
entire universe:

1. Its base with its street—Rev. 21:18b, 21b:

   a. God the Father in His nature (2 Pet. 1:4),
   signified by the pure gold, is the base on
   which this organic building is built.

   b. The street is a part of the base, indicating
   that God the Father's nature is the street
   (way—John 14:6) which has no turns or
   corners but is a circling (eternal) spiral,
   leading up to and joining with the throne of
   God at the top of the city, out of which issues
   this organic building's administration and
   its supply—Rev. 22:1-2; cf. II. I. 4. a. 3).

2. Its gates with its availability—21:12b-13, 21a:

   a. The Old Testament saints, signified by the
   pearls, produced by God the Son through
   His redeeming and life-releasing death and
   His life-dispensing resurrection, are the gates:

      1) An oyster (Christ) lives in the salty water
      (the world of death) and is wounded by a
      grain of sand (crucified for the sinner) to
      produce a pearl by secreting its life juice
      (dispensing His life element).

      2) The gates are in the number of twelve
      (eternal completion and perfection in
      administration), which is composed of
      three (the Triune God) times (mingles)
      four (man as God's creature), signifying
      that the Triune God mingles with man as
      His creature for His administration to
      accomplish His economy.

      3) The twelve gates are on the four (man as
      God's creature) sides of the organic
      building, three (the Triune God) on each
      side, signifying the availability of this

organic building toward mankind universally.

b. The twelve gates bear the names of the twelve tribes of Israel, indicating that the entry of the twelve gates, which is the entry of the entire building, is according to the requirements of Israel's law, which conducts the believers in Christ to Christ (Gal. 3:24), and that the Old Testament saints are constituents of this organic building, to be the initial section of this building for the establishment of its entry for the saints to participate in this organic building as God's good pleasure and His ultimate goal.

In the previous three chapters we covered mainly the God-men, the new man, the new creation, the Body of Christ, the overcomers, and, in a simple way, the New Jerusalem. In this chapter we will begin to consider the New Jerusalem in a detailed way, pointing out the significance of the New Jerusalem and giving a definition and interpretation of the glorious New Jerusalem.

Bible teachers have had different ways of interpreting the New Jerusalem. Mainly there are two ways: according to the letter and according to the spiritual significance. Some good Bible teachers insist that everything in the book of Revelation should be interpreted according to the letter. In keeping with such a literal interpretation, the seven golden lampstands in chapter one should be regarded not as signs or symbols but as actual physical lampstands. Likewise, the New Jerusalem should be regarded literally as a material city. For a period of time, we tried to interpret the New Jerusalem in a literal way, but eventually we came to realize that this was not the right way. Then the Lord led us to interpret the New Jerusalem according to its intrinsic spiritual significance.

The book of Revelation itself indicates that we should interpret the New Jerusalem not according to the letter but as a sign: "The revelation of Jesus Christ which God gave to Him to show to His slaves the things that must quickly take place; and He made it known by *signs*" (1:1). A sign is a symbol with a spiritual significance, such as the seven lampstands, signifying the seven churches; the seven stars, signifying the messengers of the churches (v. 20); and the beast from the sea, signifying Antichrist (13:1). In 5:6 Christ is presented as a Lamb. Since Christ is not literally a lamb, the Lamb here must also be a sign. In John 1:29 Christ is called "the Lamb of God." In the typology in the Old Testament, the Passover lamb (Exo. 12:3) signifies Christ as the One offered to God for our redemption. This is the spiritual significance of the sign of the Lamb in the book of Revelation. Just as the Lamb in Revelation 5 is a sign, so the New Jerusalem in Revelation 21 and 22 is also a sign. Only when we interpret the New Jerusalem as a sign with a spiritual significance will we have a clear view and a proper understanding of the New Jerusalem.

For more than seventy years we have been trying to understand the significance of the New Jerusalem. The city itself is a sign, and the various aspects of the city, such as the street, the gates, and the wall, also are signs. Surely we should not interpret these things according to the letters. Rather, we must seek to understand the spiritual significance of the New Jerusalem in all its aspects.

I. THE GOD-MEN

We need to see how the God-men are related to the New Jerusalem.

A. The God-men Constituting the New Man to Be the Constituents of the New Jerusalem

The God-men constitute the new man to be the constituents of the New Jerusalem. The constituents of the New Jerusalem are not lifeless materials but living persons, sons born of God to be the God-men.

B. The God-men Building Up the Body of Christ for the Building of the New Jerusalem

The God-men build up the Body of Christ for the building of the New Jerusalem. We are building up something in this age—the Body of Christ—that is for something in the next age—the New Jerusalem.

As the members of the Body of Christ, we are now building up the Body of Christ. But here we need to ask a question: With what are we building? The answer is that we are building up the Body of Christ with ourselves. Of course, we are not building with the corrupted self of the fallen humanity; we are building with the self that is being renewed, transformed, and conformed and that will be glorified. Today we are building up the Body of Christ with our regenerated new man.

In today's seminaries the students are taught to build up the church with the believers as the members. This is correct, but it is not adequate. With what kind of believers should the church be built? Can the church be built with so-called believers who are still natural, fallen persons? Can people be

used as constituents for the building up of the church only
because they have had their sins forgiven by God and have
been cleansed by the blood of Jesus? No, such persons are
not sufficient for the building up of the Body of Christ.

It is crucial for us to see that God's salvation has two
aspects. We, the believers in Christ, are redeemed by the
blood of Jesus, which washes us and which is the basis for
God to forgive us and justify us. All this belongs to the
redeeming aspect of God's salvation. The other aspect of God's
salvation is the life-imparting aspect. We are saved, therefore, not only by the redeeming aspect of God's salvation but
also by the life-imparting aspect. John 19:34 tells us that
from the pierced side of the crucified Christ two substances
came out—blood and water. The blood signifies the redeeming aspect of God's salvation, and the water signifies the
life-imparting aspect. This indicates that in addition to being
redeemed we need to be regenerated. This means that we
need to have the divine life imparted into us. This not only
regenerates us but also transforms us and conforms us to the
image of Christ. The believers with whom the church is built
should be not only redeemed, forgiven, and justified persons
but also regenerated and transformed persons.

Christ's death was both a redeeming death and a life-
releasing death. The life released through His death has been
imparted, dispensed, into us in His resurrection by the Spirit.
Christ's death released the divine life from within Him, and
now the Spirit in Christ's resurrection dispenses this released
life into the believers.

We all need to realize clearly that we have been saved by
the Lord not only through His redemption but also through
His life-imparting. On the one hand, in His crucifixion Christ
died to redeem us; on the other hand, He died to release the
divine life so that it could be imparted into us as His
redeemed ones.

As we pointed out in chapter one, it was by such a death
that Christ created the new man. In order for Christ to create
the new man, He had to do something more than merely
terminate the negative things. He also had to release the
divine life from within Him so that it could be imparted into

the redeemed persons. The God-men, as this kind of men, not only constitute the new man to be the constituents of the New Jerusalem; they also build up the Body of Christ for the building of the New Jerusalem. How glorious it is that we are now building up the New Jerusalem! Are you not such a builder? We all are co-builders, building an eternal dwelling place for ourselves.

C. The God-men Becoming the Overcomers to Consummate the New Jerusalem

The God-men not only build up the Body of Christ but also become the overcomers to consummate the New Jerusalem. The consummation of the New Jerusalem requires both maturity and increase. The building up of the church as the Body of Christ needs maturity—the measure of the stature of the fullness of Christ. Otherwise, we may have the building without the consummation.

When some hear this, they may ask, "Are we building the New Jerusalem or consummating the New Jerusalem? Is not the consummation a part of building?" Yes, it is a part of building, but it is still something distinct. To illustrate the difference we may refer to the building of a meeting hall. After the building of the hall has been completed, certain things need to be added, such as electricity, in order for the hall to be consummated. In like manner, the God-men as the overcomers need to consummate the New Jerusalem.

II. THE NEW JERUSALEM

Let us now consider what the New Jerusalem is.

A. The Union and Mingling of All God's Redeemed with the Processed and Consummated Triune God

The New Jerusalem is the union and mingling of all God's redeemed through all the four ages of the forefathers, the law, grace, and the kingdom with the processed and consummated Triune God. It is thus a union and mingling of the redeemed with the redeeming God.

We are not only united to the Triune God—we are mingled with Him. We may use the digestion of food as an illustration of mingling. The food that we eat, digest, and assimilate is eventually mingled with us. Apart from such a mingling, the food could not become our element. It is by being mingled with us that the food becomes us. The Bible tells us that Christ is eatable and that we should eat Him (John 6:51, 57). To eat Him is to have Him mingled with us.

In John 15:4a the Lord Jesus said, "Abide in Me and I in you." This mutual abiding, this mutual dwelling, is a matter of coinherence. In today's Christianity, Bible teachers may use the word *coexist* but seldom use the word *coinhere*. To coexist is different from to coinhere. To coexist is to exist together at the same time. To coinhere is to exist in one another, to dwell in one another. Coinherence, being a mutual dwelling or abiding, is therefore a mingling.

The New Jerusalem is a mutual dwelling for God and His redeemed. Actually, the New Jerusalem signifies that God as the temple (Rev. 21:22) is our dwelling and that God's redeemed as His tabernacle (v. 3) are His dwelling place. From this we can see that the New Jerusalem is not only a union of the redeeming God with His redeemed people but also a mingling of God with His redeemed ones.

B. The Consummation of God's New Creation out of His Old Creation

The New Jerusalem is the consummation of God's new creation out of His old creation in the four ages from the creation of man to the end of time.

C. An Organic Constitution

The New Jerusalem, like the Body of Christ, is an organic constitution constituted with the redeeming processed and consummated Triune God and the redeemed, transformed, and glorified tripartite men as an organism of the consummated Triune God for His eternal enlargement and expression through the glorified tripartite men.

D. The Dwelling Place of the Processed and Consummated Triune God

The New Jerusalem is also the dwelling place of the

processed and consummated Triune God, signified by the tabernacle (Rev. 21:3). Revelation 21:3 says clearly that the New Jerusalem, the holy city, is the tabernacle of God. This indicates that the New Jerusalem is God's dwelling place. The tabernacle made by Moses was a type of this tabernacle (Exo. 25:8-9; Lev. 26:11). This type was first fulfilled in Christ as God's tabernacle among men (John 1:14). He was God's tabernacle. When the Lord Jesus was on earth, God dwelt in Him as a tabernacle. Eventually, the type of the tabernacle will be fulfilled in the fullest way in the New Jerusalem, which will be the enlargement of Christ as God's dwelling place.

E. The Counterpart of Christ as the Embodiment of the Triune God

The book of Revelation shows us that the New Jerusalem is the counterpart of Christ as the embodiment of the Triune God, indicated by the bride in Christ's one-thousand-year wedding day and the wife in eternity, the precursor of which is the church as the Body of Christ (21:2, 9; 19:7, 9; Eph. 5:25-32). On the wedding day the New Jerusalem will be only the bride, but in eternity the New Jerusalem will be the wife of the Lamb as the embodied God. Since the New Jerusalem is the wife of the Lamb, it would be ridiculous to say that the New Jerusalem is a material city. It would be impossible for the embodied Triune God to marry a physical city.

F. The Ultimate Consummation of the Universal Woman in Revelation 12:1

The universal woman in Revelation 12:1 is a "great sign," signifying all the people of God (note 1, second paragraph) in the first three of the four ages, the age of the forefathers, the age of the law, and the age of grace. She has a crown of twelve stars on her head, signifying God's people in the age of the forefathers; she stands on the moon, signifying God's people in the age of the law; and she is clothed with the sun, signifying the people of God in the age of grace. This is a sign of her in the great tribulation at the end of the age of grace.

The New Jerusalem, as the greatest sign, is the ultimate consummation of the universal woman in Revelation 12:1.

The New Jerusalem signifies the aggregate of all the chosen and redeemed people of God from all the four ages of the forefathers, the law, grace, and the kingdom (21:12, 14).

G. The Spreading of the Processed and Consummated Triune God through His Redeemed, Transformed, and Glorified People

The New Jerusalem is also the spreading of the processed and consummated Triune God through His redeemed, transformed, and glorified people as His increase for His eternal purpose. This spreading is illustrated by the vine with its branches in John 15. The Lord Jesus said, "I am the vine; you are the branches" (v. 5a). The branching out of the vine is the spreading of the vine. In this chapter the Lord Jesus charged us as His branches to bear fruit, that is, to produce new believers as the further spreading of the vine tree. For the spreading of the vine, we all must endeavor to help others to be regenerated to become members of Christ. Such a work is not merely a matter of winning souls but of spreading the Triune God.

H. The Reflection and Fulfillment of the Divine Revelation concerning the Garden of Eden

The New Jerusalem is also the reflection and fulfillment of the divine revelation concerning the garden of Eden.

1. The Divine Revelation concerning the Garden of Eden and the Divine Revelation concerning the New Jerusalem Reflecting Each Other

The divine revelation concerning the garden of Eden, created by the eternal Triune God, and the divine revelation concerning the New Jerusalem, builded by the processed and consummated Triune God, reflect each other.

a. The Revelation concerning the Garden of Eden, as the Beginning of the Divine Revelation in the Holy Scripture

The revelation concerning the garden of Eden, as the

beginning of the divine revelation in the Holy Scripture, contains four matters (Gen. 2:8-14, 18-24). First, there is the tree of life as the center of God's eternal economy (v. 9a). Second, verses 10 through 14 speak of a river flowing into four heads to reach the four directions of the earth. Third, at the flow of the river are three kinds of precious materials: gold, pearl, and onyx (vv. 11-12). Here these materials are scattered and not yet builded together. Fourth, there is a couple, signifying Christ and the church (vv. 18-24; Eph. 5:22-29, 32). The wife came out of the husband (signifying Christ) as a part (a rib, signifying the resurrection life of Christ) of him taken out of him in his sleep (signifying the death of Christ) by God, which part God built into a woman (signifying the church)—Gen. 2:21-22a. Then God brought the woman to the man and made her one flesh with him as her husband to be his counterpart as his increase and expression (vv. 22b-24; John 3:29a, 30; Eph. 1:23).

b. The Revelation concerning the New Jerusalem, as the Ending of the Divine Revelation in the Holy Scripture

The revelation concerning the New Jerusalem, as the ending of the divine revelation in the Holy Scripture, also contains four matters (Rev. 21:1—22:2). First, there is the tree of life as the center of God's eternal economy (22:2). Second, according to 22:1 a river of water of life flows to reach the four directions of the earth (cf. 21:13). Third, there are three kinds of precious materials: gold, pearls, and precious stones. These materials are built together into a city, the city of New Jerusalem, by the processed and consummated Triune God (21:18-21). Fourth, the entire city is a couple. The processed and consummated redeeming Triune God in Christ is the Husband. The chosen and redeemed people of the redeeming Triune God are the wife, produced by the processed and consummated Triune God through Christ's death and resurrection with the divine life of the redeeming God as the element to be His counterpart as His enlargement and expression in eternity (vv. 2, 9; Eph. 1:23; 3:19).

2. *The Central Line of the Entire Divine Revelation throughout the Entire Holy Scripture*

What is revealed in these two parts of the divine revelation in the Holy Scripture is the central line of the entire divine revelation throughout the entire Holy Scripture. This central line should be a controlling principle to our interpreting and understanding of the Holy Scripture.

I. The Unique, Divine, and Organic Building in the Entire Universe

Next, we need to see that the New Jerusalem is the unique, divine, and organic building in the entire universe. The New Jerusalem is unique; there is no building like it on earth. The New Jerusalem is also divine; that is, it has the same nature that God has. Furthermore, the New Jerusalem is organic. This means that it is living, that it is full of life. In the entire universe only the New Jerusalem is such a divine and living building.

Let us now go on to consider the different aspects of the holy city as the unique, divine, and organic building.

1. *Its Base with Its Street*

The first aspect which we should pay attention to is its base with its street (Rev. 21:18b, 21b). Some may think that I am using the word *base* to refer to the foundation of the building. No, the base is distinct from the foundation.

In understanding what the base of the New Jerusalem is, it is helpful to see that, according to Revelation 21, the New Jerusalem must be a golden mountain. The city is pure gold (v. 18), and in length, breadth, and height it is twelve thousand stadia (v. 16). Although the city has twelve gates (v. 12), it has only one street (v. 21b). I would ask you to consider how one street could reach all twelve gates. In order for the street to reach the twelve gates, the street would have to be a spiral. Starting from the throne of God and of the Lamb at the peak (22:1), the street spirals downward until it reaches each of the gates. Only by spiraling in this way could the street, which begins at the throne, reach all twelve gates, which are at the bottom. As we consider these matters, we realize that the New Jerusalem is a golden mountain.

This golden mountain is the base of the city. Some might prefer the word *site* to the word *base,* for we often speak of the site of a building. However, because a site may be much larger in area than the building constructed on it, I feel that it would not be accurate to speak of *site* instead of *base* in relation to the New Jerusalem. The holy city occupies the entire golden mountain; it is upon this mountain that the New Jerusalem is built. Actually, the New Jerusalem, a city of pure gold, does not have a site, but it does have a base.

Others might suggest that instead of the word *base* we use the word *foundation* or the word *ground.* It would be a mistake to use *foundation* instead of *base* because Revelation 21:19-20 tells us clearly that the city of New Jerusalem has twelve foundations. Hence, we should not regard the base of the city as equal to the foundation. The word *ground* is very close in meaning to *base,* but it has a different connotation, and therefore I prefer not to use it in speaking of the New Jerusalem as a divine, organic building. After much consultation I have selected *base* as the best term to use. The gates and the wall of the New Jerusalem are built upon the golden mountain as the base.

a. God the Father in His Nature Being the Base on Which This Organic Building is Built

We have pointed out that the base of the New Jerusalem is a golden mountain. This indicates that God the Father in His nature (2 Pet. 1:4), signified by the pure gold, is the base on which this organic building is built.

b. The Street Being Part of the Base

The base of the New Jerusalem and its street are joined as one. The fact that the street is a part of the base indicates that God the Father's nature is the street (way—John 14:6) which has no turns or corners but is a circling (eternal) spiral, leading up to and joining with the throne of God at the top

of the city, out of which issues this organic building's administration and its supply (Rev. 22:1-2).

The golden street signifies that the divine nature should
be our way. We should move, act, and do things according to
God's nature. This is much higher than living according to any
kind of teaching or instruction. The reason we do not participate
in certain worldly amusements should not be that we have
been taught not to participate in those things but that in our
living we are regulated by the divine nature as our way. The
reason I cannot do certain things is that I have God's holy
nature within me and that His holy nature directs me and
becomes my way.

Some Christian groups, such as the Pentecostals, charge
people to be holy according to a set of rules. For example, they
may teach the sisters that, if they would be holy, they should
not use cosmetics. This kind of holiness is not according to the
nature of God but according to the instruction of "holiness"
people. However, among us many sisters refrain from using
cosmetics not because of instructions but because of the
divine nature. Some sisters who formerly used cosmetics
spontaneously stopped using them because they were living
according to God's nature. Others have changed the way
they dress or the way they style their hair also because of
the divine nature within them. These are examples of walk-
ing on the golden street, that is, of living according to the
divine nature. Our way is God's nature, signified by the
golden street.

It is very significant that the street has no turns or corners but is a circling spiral, leading up to and joining with the
throne of God. This indicates that when we live, walk, act,
and have our being according to the divine nature within us,
this nature joins us to the throne, where God is the reigning
One and where the authority of God is. Out from the throne
of God at the top of the city two things issue forth for the
New Jerusalem as an organic building—administration and
supply. The throne signifies God's administration, and pro-
ceeding out of the throne is the river of water of life. On the
two sides of the river grows the tree of life. This signifies
the life supply.

2. *Its Gates with Its Availability*

The next aspect of this organic building is its gates with its availability (21:12b-13, 21a).

a. *The Old Testament Saints, Signified by the Pearls, Produced by God the Son through His Redeeming and Life-releasing Death and His Life-dispensing Resurrection, Being the Gates*

The Old Testament saints, signified by the pearls, produced by God the Son through His redeeming and life-releasing death and His life-dispensing resurrection, are the gates. Here we need to see that Christ's death has two functions: to redeem and to release the divine life. Many in Christianity speak only of the redeeming function of Christ's death but not of the life-releasing function. Have you ever heard that Christ's death has released the divine life so that it can be dispensed into us? Consider the illustration of a grain of wheat which falls into the ground and dies (John 12:24). In that death two things are going on simultaneously: the destruction of the shell of that grain of wheat and the release of the life from within the grain for dispensing. This corresponds to what is said in Ephesians 2:15 concerning Christ creating in Himself the new man. The creation of the new man through the death of Christ implies both the termination of our fallen humanity and the release of the divine life for dispensing. The principle is the same with what is revealed concerning the death of Christ in 1 Peter 3:18, which tells us that Christ was put to death in the flesh but was made alive in the Spirit.

1) An Oyster Producing a Pearl

A pearl is produced by an oyster. An oyster (Christ) lives in the salty water (the world of death) and is wounded by a grain of sand (crucified for the sinner) to produce a pearl by secreting its life juice (dispensing His life element). Christ lived in this world of death and eventually was wounded, crucified, for us sinners. Through this wound He released His life so that in His resurrection it could be dispensed into us to make us pearls.

2) The Gates Being in the Number of Twelve

The gates are in the number of twelve (eternal completion and perfection in administration), which is composed of three (the Triune God) times (mingles) four (man as God's creature), signifying that the Triune God mingles with man as His creature for His administration to accomplish His economy.

3) The Twelve Gates Being
on the Four Sides of the Organic Building

The twelve gates are on the four (man as God's creature) sides of the organic building, three (the Triune God) on each side, signifying the availability of this organic building toward mankind universally.

b. The Twelve Gates Bearing
the Names of the Twelve Tribes of Israel

The twelve gates bear the names of the twelve tribes of Israel. This indicates that the entry of the twelve gates, which is the entry of the entire building, is according to the requirements of Israel's law, which conducts the believers in Christ to Christ (Gal. 3:24), and that the Old Testament saints are constituents of this organic building, to be the initial section of this building for the establishment of its entry for the saints to participate in this organic building as God's good pleasure and His ultimate goal. Here we see that, as a people, Israel became the entry for the Gentile sinners to enter into God's grace. Such an entry has four directions, indicating that the entry is toward the whole world and to all the nations.

We need to be impressed with the fact that this entry is composed with the Triune God mingled with the tripartite man. Israel is the entry because they were the first ones joined to God. Having been joined to God, they then became an entry for the Gentiles to enter into God's grace. In the next chapter we will see that the wall and the foundations with the precious stones refer to the Gentile believers. The building of the New Jerusalem includes the gates and the wall. The gates are the initial building, and the wall is the completion of the building. God the Father is the base with the street; God the Son produces the pearls for the gates; and God the Spirit transforms the saints to be the precious stones for the wall. This is the Triune God mingled with the believing Israel and the believing Gentiles to produce the New Jerusalem as a unique, divine, and organic building.

CHAPTER FIVE

THE GOD-MEN AND THE NEW JERUSALEM

(2)

Scripture Reading: Rev. 21—22

OUTLINE

II. The New Jerusalem:
  I. The unique, divine, and organic building in the entire universe:
    3. Its wall with its foundations—21:12a, 14, 15b, 17-20:
      a. The New Testament believers, signified by the precious stones, consummated by God the Spirit in His transforming and building work, are the wall and its foundations— v. 18a:
        1) The wall built with jasper separates the organic building from the nations around it.
        2) The wall is the appearance of this organic building, which is the appearance of precious jasper. This is also the appearance of God (4:3), indicating that this organic building is just the expression of God shining as jasper, a most precious stone—21:11.
        3) The wall is great and high (21:12) in the measurement of one hundred forty-four cubits (twelve times twelve—21:17), indicating that this wall is for the divine

administration of this organic building,
which is twelvefold complete and perfect.

4) The foundations of the wall are also in
the number of twelve (21:14a), signifying that the foundation of the divine
administration is twelvefold complete and
perfect.

b. The twelve foundations of the wall, built
with every precious stone (21:19-20), bear
the twelve names of the twelve apostles of
the Lamb (21:14b), indicating that this precious organic building is built according to
the apostles' teaching of the New Testament
and that the New Testament believers are
the main constituents of this organic building, to be the consummated section of this
building for the building of its main structure for the saints to be built together as
God's eternal enlargement and expression.

Note: The three items mentioned above show us that
this unique, divine, and organic building is a
constitution of the processed and consummated
Triune God with His redeemed, transformed,
and glorified people.

4. Its center with its administration and supply—
22:1-2:

a. The center is the throne of God and of the
Lamb (the redeeming Triune God), which
signifies that the administration of this
organic building is:

1) Built on the base (God the Father's nature) as its foundation (cf. Righteousness
is the foundation of God's throne—Psa.
89:14).

2) Joined to the street, the communication
of which, from the throne to the gates,
signifies the execution of the administration of this organic building.

3) Flowing out the river of water of life (the

consummated life-giving Spirit, as the consummation of the consummated Triune God— John 7:38-39; 4:14) in the middle of the street, and on the two sides of the river grows the tree of life, producing twelve fruits, yielding its fruit each month (the incarnated, crucified, and resurrected Christ, as the embodiment of the consummated Triune God—Rev. 2:7; 22:14), signifying the supply of this organic building (cf. II. I. 1. b.).

b. All the points mentioned above indicate that God's nature, one of the attributes of which is righteousness, is the foundation of the throne and that out of this foundation proceeds the administration of this organic building that affords the base for the supply of this organic building. Thus, this organic building's administration and supply are all issues from the divine nature of God the Father, who is the Originator of this organic building.

5. Its temple with its dwellers—21:22:

a. The temple of this organic building is another aspect of the tabernacle of God and is the almighty God and the Lamb (the almighty redeeming God) for the eternal dwelling place of all the redeeming God's redeemed—Psa. 90:1; John 14:23.

b. This organic building as the tabernacle, mostly of the humanity of God's redeemed, is the eternal dwelling place of the Triune God; this building as the temple of God, mostly of the divinity of the redeeming God, is the eternal dwelling place of God's redeemed. This indicates that this building is a mutual abode of the redeeming God and His redeemed.

c. In this mutual abode the redeeming God as

the Father with the redeemed as the Father's many sons form a royal household.
d. In this royal divine household the sons as priests, the royal priesthood (1 Pet. 2:9), serve the Father and as kings reign over the nations as its subjects—Rev. 22:3b-5; 21:24-26; cf. II. I. 7. a.
6. Its light with its shining —21:23-24a:
a. The light of this organic building is the glory of God in the Lamb (the Redeemer) as the lamp. Therefore, this building has no need of the sun or the moon, the natural light created by God, and the lamp, the artificial light made by man, and there is no night —21:23, 25; 22:5a.
b. The glory of God as the light is in the redeeming Lamb as the lamp shining through this organic building as the light's diffuser. This indicates that the Triune God is one with His redeemed in His expression (as what is revealed by the Son in John 14:20) shining as light over the nations.
c. The nations will walk by the light of this organic building. Thus, the entire eternal kingdom of God will be under the shining of God's glory in the Redeemer through the redeemed.

In the previous chapter we covered two aspects of the New Jerusalem—its base with its street and its gates with its availability. In this chapter we will cover four additional aspects.

3. Its Wall with Its Foundations

In the New Jerusalem the base is first as the basic factor. On this basic factor the gates are built. After this, the wall with its foundations is built. With the building of the wall, the entire structure of the New Jerusalem is completed.

a. The New Testament Believers, Signified by the Precious Stones, Consummated by God the Spirit in His Transforming and Building Work, Being the Wall and Its Foundations

The New Testament believers, signified by the precious stones, consummated by God the Spirit in His transforming and building work, are the wall of the New Jerusalem and its foundations (Rev. 21:12a, 14, 15b, 17-20). The wall and its foundations are built with twelve different kinds of precious stones (vv. 18-20). The first layer of the twelve foundations is jasper. This layer is continued by the wall itself, which also is jasper. Therefore, the foundations consist of eleven kinds of precious stones plus jasper, and the wall also is jasper.

In the previous chapter I said that the twelve gates of pearl were produced by God the Son through His redeeming and life-releasing death and His life-dispensing resurrection. There I used the word *produced* because this word refers to Christ's creating work on the cross. In Ephesians 2:15 we are told that on the cross Christ created the Jews and the Gentiles in Himself into one new man. On the cross the Lord accomplished His redeeming and life-releasing death. The Lord's resurrection continued His death to dispense the divine life released through His death on the cross. The releasing of life through Christ's death and the dispensing of life through Christ's resurrection were a creating work. Hence, Christ's work on the cross was a work of creation. It is through this creating work that the pearls are produced for the gates of the New Jerusalem. However, the precious stones that constitute the wall of the New Jerusalem and its foundations are not created but consummated by God the Spirit's transforming and building work.

Some may ask why we say that the Old Testament saints are the gates and the New Testament believers are the walls and the foundations. First, the twelve gates have the names of the twelve tribes of Israel inscribed on them (Rev. 21:12). Surely the twelve tribes here refer to the genuine Israelites, who represent all the Old Testament saints. On the wall's twelve foundations the twelve names of the apostles are inscribed, the twelve apostles representing the New Testament believers. The wall is the main part of the city. When we see the city, we see the wall first. Then we look for the gates, which are needed for entering into the city. First we enter into the city; then we are built into the wall. This signifies that the genuine Israelites of the twelve tribes were the first ones who entered into God's New Testament economy. They were the first ones to participate in God's grace. In other words, they were the first ones who entered into Christ. Thus, they became the child-conductors to conduct others into Christ (Gal. 3:24), and then they became the entrance. In this intrinsic sense, the Old Testament saints are the gates for others to enter into Christ. Through the transforming work of the Spirit, those who have entered into Christ through the gates become precious stones to build up the wall.

Formerly in my ministry I did not say that the pearls signify the Old Testament saints as the entrance for people to enter into God's New Testament economy, and I did not say that the precious stones signify the New Testament believers as the majority for the main structure of the city. I received this light very recently.

To interpret the Bible is not an easy thing. This does not mean that those who are the pearls have only the experience of the pearl, that is, that they have only the experience of Christ's death and resurrection and do not need to have the experience of the Spirit's transformation. Neither does it mean that those who are the precious stones and have the experience of the Spirit's transformation do not need to have the experience of Christ's death and resurrection. We need to realize that the Old Testament saints and the New Testament believers are one entity. As one entity, they pass through Christ's death and resurrection, and then they go on to pass through the Spirit's transformation.

The entire New Testament teaches us that we, the people of God who are the God-men, need to be redeemed and to have the divine life that was released through Christ's death imparted into us in His resurrection. Then we need to go on to experience the transforming work of the Holy Spirit, through which we become the precious materials. In 1 Corinthians 3:12 Paul spoke of both silver (corresponding to the pearls in Revelation 21:21) and precious stones, but he did not designate some believers as silver (pearls) and others as precious stones. In other words, on the one hand, we are pearls; on the other hand, we are precious stones. Thus, the Old Testament saints can claim that they are pearls as well as precious stones, and the New Testament believers can claim that they are precious stones as well as pearls.

1) The Wall Built with Jasper Separating the Organic Building from the Nations around It

The wall of the New Jerusalem built with jasper separates the organic building from the nations around it. The first function of the wall is to separate. The second function of the wall is to provide protection. A person may build a wall around his house to separate it and to protect it from the outside environment. In a similar way, the wall of the New Jerusalem separates the city from the nations around it and fully protects the interests of God within the city.

2) The Wall Being the Appearance of This Organic Building

The wall is the appearance of this organic building, which is the appearance of precious jasper. This is also the appearance of God (4:3), indicating that this organic building is just the expression of God shining as jasper, a most precious stone (21:11). When we look at the city, we first see the appearance of the wall, which is the appearance of precious jasper. The entire wall is built with jasper. Thus, the appearance of the wall is the appearance of jasper. This is also the appearance of God, for in Revelation 4:3 we are told that the very God sitting on the throne looks like a jasper stone. This is very meaningful. The jasper God within the city is expressed by the jasper wall. Hence, the two are one. This indicates that the New Jerusalem is the expression of God.

According to Revelation 21:11 the shining of the New Jerusalem is the shining of jasper. The wall of the New Jerusalem is jasper, and God as the content of the city is also jasper. Both the wall and God shine as jasper. The color of jasper is dark green. In typology green signifies life, and dark green signifies life in its richness. Our God is the totality of life. Hence, in His appearance He is dark green. Revelation 4:3 also says that He looks like a sardius, a red precious stone. This indicates that God is also the redeeming God. He is not only a God full of life, but He is also the redeeming God.

3) The Wall Being Great and High in the Measurement of One Hundred Forty-four Cubits

The wall of the New Jerusalem is great and high (21:12) in the measurement of one hundred forty-four cubits (twelve times twelve—v. 17), indicating that this wall is for the divine administration of this organic building, which is twelvefold complete and perfect. The city proper of New Jerusalem is like a mountain with a length, breadth, and height of twelve thousand stadia (v. 16), whereas the wall itself, from the foundation to the top, has a height of one hundred forty-four cubits. The number twelve signifies absolute perfection and eternal completion in God's administration. There are three aspects to the significance of the number twelve: the aspect of being eternal, the aspect of being complete, and the aspect of being perfect. Thus, this number signifies that God's administration is eternal, complete, and perfect, unlike man's administration, which is neither eternal nor complete nor perfect. One hundred forty-four is twelve times twelve, indicating that the divine administration of the New Jerusalem as God's organic building is twelvefold eternal, complete, and perfect. How perfect and complete is the wall of the holy city in God's eternal administration!

4) The Foundations of the Wall
Being Also in the Number of Twelve

The foundations of the wall are also in the number of twelve (v. 14a), signifying that the foundation of the divine administration is twelvefold complete and perfect. Thus, the foundations are the same as the wall. Both are for God to administrate, to govern, the city.

b. The Twelve Foundations of the Wall,
Built with Every Precious Stone, Bearing
the Twelve Names of the Twelve Apostles of the Lamb

The twelve foundations of the wall, built with every precious stone (vv. 19-20), bear the twelve names of the twelve apostles of the Lamb (v. 14b), indicating that this precious organic building is built according to the apostles' teaching of the New Testament and that the New Testament believers are the main constituents of this organic building, to be the consummated section of this building for the building of its main structure for the saints to be built together as God's eternal enlargement and expression. The twelve tribes of Israel represent the law of the Old Testament, whereas the twelve apostles of the Lamb represent the apostles' teaching of the New Testament. The gates of the New Jerusalem are the initial section of the building, and the wall is the consummated section.

The three items mentioned above—the base with the street, the gates, and the wall with its foundations—show us that this unique, divine, and organic building is a constitution of the processed and consummated Triune God with His redeemed, transformed, and glorified people. The first item, the base of the city, is a figure signifying God the Father in His nature. God the Father is the first person of the Trinity. The gates of pearl signify the creation produced by God the Son, who is the second person of the Trinity. The wall and its foundations of precious stones signifies the transforming and building work of the Holy Spirit, who is the third person

of the Divine Trinity. Thus, in these first three items we have
God the Father, God the Son, and God the Spirit. Moreover, on
the gates there are the names of the twelve tribes of Israel,
indicating the Old Testament saints, and on the foundations
there are the names of the twelve apostles, signifying the
New Testament saints. Hence, we have the Triune God
mingled with all the saints, who are God's redeemed, transformed, and glorified people.

4. Its Center with Its Administration and Supply

The city of New Jerusalem is built on a golden mountain
with gates and with a wall and its foundations. This is the
complete building. This consummated building has a center,
the throne of God and of the Lamb (22:1). This throne as the
center of the city surely is on the top of the city, the top of
the golden mountain.

a. The Center Being the Throne of God
and of the Lamb (the Redeeming Triune God)

The center of the city is the throne of God and of the Lamb
(the redeeming Triune God). The two, God and the Lamb,
signify the redeeming Triune God. The redeeming God is both
God and the Lamb.

1) Built on the Base (God the Father's Nature)
as Its Foundation

The throne signifies the administration of the New
Jerusalem. This signifies that the administration of this
organic building is built on the base (God the Father's nature)
as its foundation. Psalm 89:14 says that righteousness is the
foundation of God's throne. This implies that the very nature
of God as the foundation of God's administration refers, in
this aspect, to God's attribute of righteousness. God has a
nature, and His nature is of many attributes, which include
love, light, holiness, righteousness, kindness, etc. All these
divine virtues are the attributes of God. Among all these
divine attributes, the most important is righteousness. This is
why we need to be saved according to God's righteousness
(Rom. 1:16-17; 3:21-22). If we are saved only according to

God's grace or according to God's love, our salvation is not legally justified; it is not judicial. Anything that is of righteousness is judicial, is legal, according to the law.

The foundation of God's throne is not grace or love. Such a foundation would not be sure to us. God's throne is established on righteousness as its foundation. This righteousness is the main attribute in God's nature. In the New Jerusalem both the street and the base are gold, signifying God's nature in the attribute of righteousness. This is the foundation of the throne of God.

2) Joined to the Street

The administration of this organic building is also joined to the street, the communication of which, from the throne to the gates, signifies the execution of the administration of this organic building. In the New Jerusalem there is a street that is joined to the throne. The street is for communication. The street joined to the throne is for the governmental dealings, that is, the administration, in the New Jerusalem.

3) Flowing Out the River of Water of Life, on the Two Sides of Which the Tree of Life Grows

The administration in the New Jerusalem as the divine, organic building flows out the river of water of life (the consummated life-giving Spirit, as the consummation of the consummated Triune God—John 7:38-39; 4:14) in the middle of the street, and on the two sides of the river grows the tree of life, producing twelve fruits, yielding its fruit each month (the incarnated, crucified, and resurrected Christ, as the embodiment of the consummated Triune God—Rev. 2:7; 22:14), signifying the supply of this organic building (cf. section II. I. 1. b. in Chapter Four).

In the middle of the street flows the river of water of life, and on the two sides of the river grows the tree of life (vv. 1-2). The river of water of life signifies the consummated life-giving Spirit, and the tree of life signifies the incarnated, crucified, and resurrected Christ. The throne flows out the river, on the two sides of which grows the tree of life, and the river flows in the middle of the street. Thus, three things flow out of the throne: the divine administration, the river of water of life, and the tree of life. The latter two are the provision, the supply, of the holy city.

It is helpful to look at the picture of the New Jerusalem. First, there is the base of gold, and the street of gold is on the base. The street and the base are one piece of gold. At the top end of the street is the throne of God. Thus, the street comes out from the throne. In the middle of the street the river of life flows. Hence, the river of life also flows out of the throne. On the sides of the river the tree of life grows. The river of water of life and the tree of life are the supply of the city. This indicates that the administration of the city and the supply of the city all flow out of the throne, on which God and the Lamb, the redeeming God, are sitting.

This picture indicates that the redeeming God is the very source. From His righteousness as one of the attributes of His nature issues out the administration of His organic building, which is joined to the street. Furthermore, from His throne flows out the river of water of life, which grows the tree of life to be the life supply as the provision to supply the entire city. Thus, in this picture we have the administration, the provision, and also the communication, the street. All these come from God in His righteous nature. In summary, the base and the street are joined together as one piece of gold. At the top end of the street is the throne of God, and the redeeming God is sitting upon the throne as the source, from whom flows out the administration, the communication, and the provision of the city. This is the way to interpret such a picture.

The city of New Jerusalem is built with large, tall gates, and it also has its center. If there were no communication, no street, and if there were no administration and no provision of food and water, how could the city live? In the New Jerusalem the throne flows out the water, and the water grows the tree of life, which produces twelve kinds of fruit as the food. These three things—the administration, the communication, and the life supply—flow out of the God of righteousness to take care of the city.

b. Out of God's Nature as the Foundation of His Throne
Proceeding the Administration That Affords
the Base for the Supply of the City

All the points mentioned above indicate that God's nature, one of the attributes of which is righteousness, is the foundation of the throne and that out of this foundation proceeds the administration of this organic building that affords the base for the supply of this organic building. Thus, the administration and supply of the New Jerusalem are all issues from the divine nature of God the Father, who is the Originator of this organic building.

The administration affords the base for the supply of the city. If there were no proper administration in the city of Anaheim, who would take care of the daily water supply? Anaheim has an adequate supply of water because it has a strong government. The administration of the government is the base to supply the city with water.

The picture of the throne joined to the street flowing out the administration, the communication, and the supply shows us that the divine administration is from the throne of God, the divine communication goes along with the divine administration, and the divine supply comes from the divine administration and the divine communication under the authority of God's throne. This indicates that if we want to participate in the divine supply in the New Jerusalem, we must submit ourselves to God's throne of authority and to His divine administration and take care of the divine communication in the entire city of New Jerusalem.

5. Its Temple with Its Dwellers

We have seen the base, the gates, the wall, and the center of the New Jerusalem. It would seem that these things are sufficient. But who are the dwellers of the city? And what is the dwelling place of the dwellers? Revelation 21:22 says, "And I saw no temple in it, for the Lord God the Almighty and the Lamb are its temple." This verse says that there is no temple in the city, because God and the Lamb (the redeeming God) are the temple. Only the Holy Spirit could write in such a way. In verse 3 the city is called "the tabernacle of God." The temple and the tabernacle are actually one. The tabernacle was God's portable, movable building, a building that traveled in the wilderness. When the tabernacle became the temple, it was settled, no longer portable. God was in the tabernacle when the children of Israel were traveling for forty years in the wilderness. Thus, the tabernacle was God's temple (1 Sam. 3:3). Within the tabernacle were the Holy of Holies and the Holy Place. When the children of Israel entered into the good land, they built the temple to replace the tabernacle. Within the temple also were the Holy of Holies and the Holy Place. The temple is not only the place where God stays to be worshipped but also the place where those who serve God live. Those who serve God live in the temple and take the temple as their dwelling.

a. The Temple of This Organic Building
Being Another Aspect of the Tabernacle of God
and Being the Almighty God and the Lamb
(the Almighty Redeeming God)

The temple of this organic building is another aspect of the tabernacle of God and is the almighty God and the Lamb (the almighty redeeming God) for the eternal dwelling place of all of the redeeming God's redeemed (Psa. 90:1; John 14:23). The temple is God's dwelling place, but it becomes the place where God's serving ones, the priests, live. Hence, the priests live together with God. The temple is God Himself. Thus, the very God worshipped by the priests is the dwelling place of the priests.

In Psalm 90:1 Moses wrote, "Lord, Thou hast been our dwelling place in all generations." Then, in Deuteronomy 33:27 he said, "The eternal God is thy dwelling-place" (ASV). Even in the Old Testament, Moses considered God as Israel's dwelling place. Later, Israel, under God's punishment, was scattered among the Gentile nations. In Ezekiel 11:16 God said to them that in their dispersion He would be their sanctuary. Moreover, in the New Testament John 14:23 says that the Father and the Son will come to the one who loves the Son and make an abode, a dwelling place, with him. This dwelling place will be a mutual abode for the Father and the Son and the Son's lover. When a young couple is going to be married, the young man may tell his bride that he will purchase a house that will be a mutual dwelling place for them as husband and wife. Eventually, the husband is the abode to the wife, and the wife is the abode to the husband. In the same way, God is an abode to us, and we are an abode to Him. The New Jerusalem will be a mutual dwelling place for God and His redeemed.

b. This Organic Building as the Tabernacle and the Temple Being a Mutual Dwelling Place of the Redeeming God and His Redeemed

This organic building as the tabernacle, mostly of the humanity of God's redeemed, is the eternal dwelling place of the Triune God; this building as the temple of God, mostly of the divinity of the redeeming God, is the eternal dwelling place of God's redeemed. This indicates that this building is a mutual abode of the redeeming God and His redeemed.

The tabernacle is built mostly with the humanity of God's people to be God's dwelling place. The temple is built mostly of divinity to be the dwelling place of God's redeemed. This indicates that God takes us as His dwelling place and gives Himself to us to be our dwelling place. The divine God lives in a human tabernacle, and the human redeemed live in a divine dwelling place. This indicates the mingling of divinity with humanity, in which both humanity and divinity became a mutual abode. Concerning God and His redeemed in the New Jerusalem, a new hymn says, "As man yet God, they coinhere, / A mutual dwelling place to be." The New Jerusalem as the tabernacle of God indicates that the redeemed of God are the dwelling place of God, and the redeeming God as the temple indicates that God is the dwelling place for His serving ones.

c. In This Mutual Abode the Redeeming God as the Father with the Redeemed as the Father's Many Sons Forming a Royal Household

In this mutual abode, where both God and His redeemed

abide, the redeeming God as the Father with the redeemed as
the Father's many sons form a royal household.

d. In This Royal Divine Household the Sons
as Priests, the Royal Priesthood, Serving the Father and
as Kings Reigning over the Nations as Its Subjects

In this royal divine household the sons as priests, the
royal priesthood (1 Pet. 2:9), serve the Father and as kings
reign over the nations as its subjects (Rev. 22:3b-5; 21:24-26;
cf. section II. I. 7. a. in Chapter Six).

6. Its Light with Its Shining

Thus far we have considered the base with the street, the
gates, the wall of the city with its foundations, the center for
the administration and the supply of the city, and the temple
where God's serving ones, the priests, dwell. In constructing a
house, the last thing is to install the electrical wires to bring
in light. As the divine, organic building, the New Jerusalem
has its light with its shining (vv. 23-24a).

a. The Light of This Organic Building Being
the Glory of God in the Lamb (the Redeemer) as the Lamp

The light of this organic building is the glory of God in
the Lamb (the Redeemer) as the lamp (v. 23b). Therefore, this
building has no need of the sun or the moon, the natural
light created by God, and the lamp, the artificial light made
by man, and there is no night (vv. 23a, 25; 22:5a). In the
New Jerusalem God is the light and Christ is the lamp.
Although there will be no night there, there is still the need of
light. However, the light is not the created light or the artificial light made by man, but God Himself in the Lamb as the
lamp.

b. The Glory of God as the Light
Being in the Redeeming Lamb as the Lamp Shining
through This Organic Building as the Light's Diffuser

The glory of God as the light is in the redeeming Lamb as
the lamp shining through this organic building as the light's
diffuser. This indicates that the Triune God is one with His

redeemed in His expression (as what is revealed by the Son in John 14:20) shining as light over the nations. In the New Jerusalem there are the light, the lamp, and the diffuser to shine the divine light out. In John 14:20 the Lord said to His disciples, "In that day you will know that I am in My Father, and you in Me, and I in you." This shows that the light is in the lamp, and the lamp is in the diffuser. The light is God the Father, the lamp is God the Son, and the diffuser is the Body of Christ, the New Jerusalem, to shine the divine light over the nations, the peoples who live around the New Jerusalem.

c. The Nations Walking by the Light of This Organic Building

The nations will walk by the light of this organic building. Thus, the entire eternal kingdom of God will be under the shining of God's glory in the Redeemer through the redeemed as the diffuser. The eternal kingdom of God includes the New Jerusalem and the nations around it. The redeemed who constitute the New Jerusalem are the kings to reign, and the nations around the New Jerusalem are the subjects.

CHAPTER SIX

THE GOD-MEN AND THE NEW JERUSALEM

(3)

Scripture Reading: Rev. 21—22

OUTLINE

II. The New Jerusalem:
  I. The unique, divine, and organic building in the entire universe:
    7. Its reign with its subjects—21:24, 26, 3-4; 22:2b:
      a. The divine royal household, as kings under the Father as the King of kings, reign within this organic building (22:3b-5) over the nations around it as its subjects (21:24, 26; cf. II. I. 5. d.). This forms the eternal kingdom of the Lord God and of His Christ (11:15; Eph. 5:5; Gal. 5:21; 2 Pet. 1:11; John 3:3, 5). Their kind of reign began with the God-men as the overcomers in the millennial kingdom (Rev. 2:26-27).
      b. The subjects are the people who were created by God but fell.
      c. They were recovered back to their original condition according to God's creation, that is, redeemed by God with the death of Christ (Heb. 2:9; Col. 1:20) but not regenerated by God with the life of Christ (1 Pet. 1:3; John 3:3, 5, 15).
      d. They are the sheep, the righteous of the

nations, justified by Christ at His throne of
glory in His coming back (according to the
eternal gospel, not the gospel of grace,
preached by an angel during the great tribulation—Rev. 14:6-7) that they may inherit
the kingdom (prepared by God for them
from the foundation of the world), that
is, enter into eternal life—to participate in
(the eternal blessing of) the eternal life—
Matt. 25:31-40, 46.

e. They will be God's peoples, among whom is
the tabernacle of God—Rev. 21:3.

f. They will be sustained to live the human
life for eternity by the leaves of the tree of
life (22:2b), signifying the deeds of Christ,
but they will not eat of the fruit of the tree
of life, which is for God's redeemed as His
sons (21:7).

g. They will walk in the light of this organic
building (21:24a), which is the glory of God
shining in the Lamb through His redeemed,
in their relationship with God, and they will
also live under the light of the sun created
by God and the lamp made by man in their
human affairs.

h. The earthly kings of the subjects will bring
their splendor to God (21:24b), as the twenty-
four elders cast their crowns before the
throne of God (4:10), and the nations will
bring their splendor and their honor, that is,
their preciousness in status and dignity in
position, to God (21:26), as the four living
creatures do to God, who sits upon the
throne (4:9).

i. God will wipe away every tear from their
eyes; and death will be no more, nor will
there be sorrow or crying or pain anymore;
for the former things have passed away—
21:4.

J. The New Jerusalem as such a marvelous, wonderful, and amazing entity is:
   1. The aggregate of all the visions and revelations in the Holy Scripture.
   2. The total accomplishment of the types, figures, and shadows, and the total fulfillment of the prophecies of the Holy Scripture.
   3. The final conclusion of the sixty-six books of the Holy Scripture.
K. This New Jerusalem as the organism of God is:
   1. His good pleasure of His heart's desire—Eph. 1:5, 9.
   2. God's ultimate goal.
   3. The complete fulfillment of the eternal economy of God—Eph. 1:10; 3:9.
L. Such a New Jerusalem is the total blessing of the eternal life (Matt. 19:29; Rom. 5:21) that all the redeemed people of God will enjoy in Christ as the unsearchable blessing of God's dynamic and complete salvation for their eternal inheritance.
M. This excellent and lovely New Jerusalem, not the "heavenly mansion" as the superstition of millions of Christians, is the dear expectation of God's elect (Heb. 11:10) and the destination, the goal, of the heavenly pilgrims.
N. In the new heaven and new earth (the eternal kingdom of God), in which is the New Jerusalem, righteousness will dwell for eternity—2 Pet. 3:13:
   1. God's divine work throughout the four ages of man, the age of the forefathers, the age of law, the age of grace, and the age of the kingdom, on the one hand, consummates His new creation, and on the other hand, does away with Satan, sin, the old creation, and the old man to clear up all the unrighteousness from the universe.
   2. Then, in the new heaven and new earth, that is, in the eternal kingdom of God, righteousness will dwell, which is one of the attributes of God

and the foundation of God (Psa. 89:14) and
issues in peace. Such a righteousness is suitable for God to express Himself in the New
Jerusalem, as His royal household, to the
nations as His subjects.

O. It is according to these five items J to N that the
grace of the Lord Jesus Christ is always with all
the saints from the age of grace through the age of
the kingdom to eternity for the accomplishment of
the eternal economy of God—Rev. 22:21.

The more I engage in the crystallization-study of the New Jerusalem as it is unveiled in Revelation 21 and 22, the more I worship God for His revelation. Only He, the omnipotent and omniscient One, could write such a word.

Before we consider further aspects of the New Jerusalem, I would like to review the main points we have covered thus far regarding the New Jerusalem as the unique, divine, and organic building in the entire universe. We have seen that the New Jerusalem itself is of six aspects: its base with its street; its gates with its availability; its wall with its foundations; its center with its administration and supply; its temple with its dwellers; and its light with its shining. In reviewing these matters I am burdened to point out that every aspect of the New Jerusalem as an organic building is nothing other than the Triune God as the redeeming God with His chosen, redeemed, regenerated, transformed, and glorified people. It is crucial that we see this.

Of the six aspects, the first three—the base, the gates, and the wall—are a group. The base with its street, the gates, and the wall are for the complete building on the base. Without the base there could not be a building. As an illustration of what we mean by *base* we may refer to the building of a house in the housing development called Grace Gardens in Anaheim. Before we were allowed to build a house on the site, we first had to build the base of the house. The base is not the building site but the ground under the foundation of the house. This ground, this base, must be strong enough to support the house. The base, therefore, is the ground under the house that has been prepared, strengthened, and reinforced to bear the weight of the building. Just as a house in Grace Gardens has a base, so the New Jerusalem has a base. The base of the New Jerusalem is a golden mountain. The street of the city, which is part of the base, is also gold. Gold signifies God the Father, the First of the Trinity, in His nature. This indicates that the divine nature is both the base and the street of the New Jerusalem.

The pearl gates are produced by God the Son, the Second of the Trinity, through His redeeming and life-releasing death and His life-dispensing resurrection. This indicates that Christ created the New Jerusalem through His terminating, redeeming, and life-releasing death and His life-dispensing resurrection. In brief, Christ created the New Jerusalem through His death and resurrection and with Himself as the element. According to Ephesians 2:15 on the cross Christ created the new man in Himself, that is, with Himself as the element. In Ephesians 2:15 "in Himself" indicates that Christ is the element with which the new man was created. Christ created the New Jerusalem through His death, which is joined to His resurrection.

After the creation of the New Jerusalem, there is the need of consummation, which is related to the wall with its foundations. This points to the Spirit, the Third of the Trinity, in His transforming and building work. Now we have the complete building, consisting of the base with its street, the gates, and the wall with its foundations.

We need to see that this complete building is built by the Triune God with each of the three of the Trinity being something. God the Father in His nature is the base and the street; God the Son in His death and resurrection and with Himself as the element produces the gates; and God the Spirit in His transforming and building work builds up the wall with its foundations. But what are the materials for this building? Ephesians 2:15 reveals that the materials are "the two," the Jews and the Gentiles, whom Christ created "in Himself into one new man." For this reason the gates bear the twelve names of the twelve tribes of Israel, signifying the Old Testament saints, and the foundations of the wall bear the names of the twelve apostles, signifying the New Testament believers. Therefore, the Old Testament saints and the New Testament saints are the materials.

In the New Jerusalem we have God the Father in His nature as the base and the street, God the Son as the Creator through His death and resurrection and with Himself as the element producing the gates, God the Spirit with His transforming and building work building the wall with its foundations, and the Old and New Testament saints as the materials. When we put all this together, we have the mingling of the processed and consummated Triune God with His chosen, redeemed, regenerated, transformed, and glorified people. This is the New Jerusalem.

How can the materials, from both the Old Testament and the New Testament, be consummated and built to become the New Jerusalem? The answer to this question is that we must pass through the death and resurrection of Christ to have our fallen humanity terminated and to have our original, God-created humanity redeemed and recovered so that Christ can use us as the materials. Through the death of Christ on the cross, our fallen humanity was terminated and our original humanity was redeemed that the divine life released in His death could be dispensed into this redeemed humanity. Then in Christ's resurrection the Spirit dispenses the released divine life into the redeemed humanity to regenerate us. This is the creation of the New Jerusalem. Now, in the consummation, the regenerating Spirit works as the sanctifying, renewing, transforming, conforming, and glorifying Spirit to consummate the entire building.

I hope that through this review you will have a clear view of what the New Jerusalem is. The New Jerusalem is the mingling of the processed and consummated Triune God with the believers through Christ's death and resurrection and the Spirit's regenerating, sanctifying, renewing, transforming, conforming, and glorifying work.

This consummated building is now ready for use, but it still needs certain furnishings. The first item of the furnishings of the New Jerusalem is the throne of God and the Lamb as its center. This throne is joined to the street, on which flows the river of life with the tree of life as the supply. With the street we have the communication for administration, and with the river we have the water of life and the fruit of the tree of life for supply. The water of life is for drinking and the fruit of the tree of life is for eating. This is a matter of provision. For administration this throne is the throne of authority, and for provision this throne is the throne of grace. Hebrews 4:16 tells us that we may come to the throne of grace to "receive mercy and find grace for timely help." If there were not such a throne, then in the New Jerusalem there would be no administration, no communication, no food, and no water. Thus, there is the need of the throne as the first item of the furnishings.

The second item is the sanctuary, the temple. The redeeming God Himself is the temple in which His priests live and where they serve Him. The throne is for administration and provision, and the sanctuary is our dwelling place and our serving place.

The last of the furnishings is the light with its shining. The glory of God as the light is in the redeeming Lamb as the lamp.

The three furnishings all involve the Triune God. The Triune God is the basic structure of the building, and the Triune God becomes the redeeming God who possesses the throne, who is the sanctuary, and who is the lamp with the light. The structure is the Triune God, and the furnishings are the redeeming God. This is the New Jerusalem, and this is also us. To be parts of the New Jerusalem, we need to be created, consummated, and furnished with the Triune God and the redeeming God.

To be constituted into such persons is not merely to be improved, remodeled, or changed. No matter how much a natural person is improved, remodeled, or changed, he is still a natural person, not a God-man like Jesus Christ. Christ is the God-man who is now producing many God-men to be created, consummated, and furnished to be the New Jerusalem. If we see that we are part of this New Jerusalem, we will see what kind of person we should be today. We should not be a good man like Confucius or Socrates. Rather, we should be a God-man for the New Jerusalem. We all need to see this.

Let us now go on to consider another matter related to the New Jerusalem as the unique, organic building.

7. *Its Reign with Its Subjects*

The New Jerusalem also has its reign with its subjects (Rev. 21:24, 26, 3-4; 22:2b). It has been created, consummated, and furnished for the purpose of reigning.

THE GOD-MEN AND THE NEW JERUSALEM 97

*a. The Divine Royal Household as the Kings Reigning
over the Nations around It as Its Subjects*

The New Jerusalem is a divine royal household, as kings under the Father as the King of kings, reigning within this organic building (22:3b-5) over the nations around it as its subjects (21:24, 26). This forms the eternal kingdom of the Lord God and of His Christ (11:15; Eph. 5:5; Gal. 5:21; 2 Pet. 1:11; John 3:3, 5). Their kind of reign began with the God-men as the overcomers in the millennial kingdom (Rev. 2:26-27).

*b. The Subjects Being the People
Who Were Created by God but Fell*

The subjects of the reign of the New Jerusalem are the people who were created by God but fell.

*c. The Subjects Being Recovered Back
to Their Original Condition according to God's Creation*

The subjects have been recovered back to their original condition according to God's creation, that is, redeemed by God with the death of Christ (Heb. 2:9; Col. 1:20) but not regenerated by God with the life of Christ (1 Pet. 1:3; John 3:3, 5, 15).

*d. The Subjects Being the Sheep Justified by Christ
at His Throne of Glory in His Coming Back*

The subjects are the sheep, the righteous of the nations, justified by Christ at His throne of glory in His coming back. They are justified not according to the gospel of grace but according to the eternal gospel preached by an angel during the great tribulation (Rev. 14:6-7). They have been justified that they may inherit the kingdom prepared by God for them from the foundation of the world, that is, enter into eternal life—to participate in the eternal blessing of the eternal life (Matt. 25:31-40, 46).

During the three and a half years of the great tribulation, Antichrist, the Caesar of the revived Roman Empire, and the false prophet will be instigated by Satan to fight against Christ. Whereas the Father, the Son, and the Holy Spirit form a divine Trinity, Satan, Antichrist, and the false prophet will form a demonic trinity. The believers who remain on earth after the rapture of the overcomers will suffer persecution under Antichrist. During that time an angel will preach the eternal gospel, telling the people on earth to fear God and worship Him. To persecute the saints is not to fear God, and to worship the image of Antichrist is not to worship God. The angel who preaches the eternal gospel, therefore, will be telling the people not to persecute God's people. Those who receive this gospel will fear God and love the persecuted people of God. Thus, the Lord Jesus will say that what they did in caring for the least of His brothers, they did to Him (Matt. 25:35-40). Based upon their good conduct and upon their receiving the eternal gospel, He will justify them and regard them as the sheep. However, the Lord Jesus will regard the rest as goats and condemn them, telling them to go into the eternal fire (vv. 41-46a). The righteous, the sheep, on the contrary, will go into eternal life (v. 46b). They will not receive eternal life but will go into the environment, the condition, and the situation of the eternal life. These sheep will become the nations as the subjects of the reign of the New Jerusalem in the new heaven and new earth.

e. The Subjects Being God's Peoples

These subjects will be God's peoples, among whom is the tabernacle of God. Revelation 21:3 speaks not of the sons of God (vv. 6-7) but of the peoples of God, who will be the nations around the New Jerusalem.

f. The Subjects Being Sustained to Live the Human Life for Eternity

The subjects of the reign of the New Jerusalem will be sustained to live the human life for eternity by the leaves of the tree of life (22:2b), signifying the deeds of Christ, but they will not eat of the fruit of the tree of life, which is for God's redeemed as His sons (21:7). This means that the subjects will not be regenerated; that is, they will not have eternal life but only the life of the humanity that was originally created by God and then was redeemed and recovered.

Although they will not have eternal life, they will live for eternity by the leaves of the tree of life.

The fruit of the tree of life will be our food to nourish us in the New Jerusalem, but the leaves of the tree of life, which are good not for eating but for medicine, will be for the healing of the nations. Because the leaves are effective for healing, the nations will live forever. The leaves of the tree of life symbolize the deeds of Christ. The regenerated believers will eat of the fruit of the tree of life, receiving Christ as their inward life and life supply that they may enjoy the divine life for eternity, whereas the restored nations will be healed by the leaves of the tree of life, taking the deeds of Christ as their outward guide and regulation that they may live the human life for eternity.

g. The Subjects Walking in the Light of This Organic Building

In their relationship with God, the subjects will walk in the light of this organic building (v. 24a), which is the glory of God shining in the Lamb through His redeemed. This means that in matters related to God the nations as the subjects will walk in the divine light. For their human affairs they will also live under the light of the sun created by God and the lamp made by man.

h. The Earthly Kings of the Subjects Bringing Their Splendor to God

The earthly kings of the subjects will bring their splendor, that is, their glory, to God (21:24b), as the twenty-four elders cast their crowns before the throne of God (4:10). The nations will bring their splendor and their honor, that is, their preciousness in status and dignity in position, to God (21:26), as the four living creatures do to God, who sits upon the throne (4:9).

i. God Wiping Away Every Tear from Their Eyes

God will wipe away every tear from their eyes; and death will be no more, nor will there be sorrow or crying or pain anymore; for the former things will have passed away (21:4).

All these are the blessings to the nations as the subjects, not to the saints as the sons of God (vv. 5-7), under the reign of the New Jerusalem.

J. The New Jerusalem as a Marvelous, Wonderful, and Amazing Entity

The New Jerusalem as such a marvelous, wonderful, and amazing entity is the aggregate of all the visions and revelations in the Holy Scripture; the total accomplishment of the types, figures, and shadows, and the total fulfillment of the prophecies of the Holy Scripture; and the final conclusion of the sixty-six books of the Holy Scripture. Without the New Jerusalem, the Bible would not have a conclusion.

K. The New Jerusalem as the Organism of God

The New Jerusalem as the organism of God is God's good pleasure of His heart's desire (Eph. 1:5, 9), God's ultimate goal, and the complete fulfillment of the eternal economy of God (v. 10; 3:9).

L. The New Jerusalem Being the Total Blessing of the Eternal Life

Such a New Jerusalem is the total blessing of the eternal life (Matt. 19:29; Rom. 5:21) that all the redeemed people of God will enjoy in Christ as the unsearchable blessing of God's dynamic and complete salvation for their eternal inheritance.

M. The New Jerusalem Being the Dear Expectation of God's Elect and the Destination of the Heavenly Pilgrims

This excellent and lovely New Jerusalem, not the "heavenly mansion" as the superstition of millions of Christians, is the dear expectation of God's elect (Heb. 11:10) and the destination, the goal, of the heavenly pilgrims. Today we are sojourners, journeying on a rugged road toward our eternal goal, the New Jerusalem.

N. Righteousness Dwelling for Eternity in the New Heaven and New Earth, in Which Is the New Jerusalem

In the new heaven and new earth (the eternal kingdom of God), in which is the New Jerusalem, righteousness will dwell for eternity (2 Pet. 3:13). This means that the entire eternal kingdom of God, including the New Jerusalem, is a matter of righteousness.

1. God's Divine Work Consummating the New Creation and Clearing Up All Unrighteousness from the Universe

God's divine work throughout the four ages of man, the age of the forefathers, the age of law, the age of grace, and the age of the kingdom, on the one hand, consummates His new creation, and on the other hand, does away with Satan, sin, the old creation, and the old man to clear up all the unrighteousness from the universe. There will no longer be any unrighteousness in the universe. Righteousness will dwell in the new heaven and new earth for eternity.

2. Righteousness Being Suitable for God to Express Himself in the New Jerusalem as His Royal Household to the Nations as His Subjects

After all unrighteousness has been cleared away from the universe, then in the new heaven and new earth, that is, in the eternal kingdom of God, righteousness will dwell. Righteousness is one of the attributes of God, is the foundation of the throne of God (Psa. 89:14), and issues in peace (Isa. 32:17). Such a righteousness is suitable for God to express Himself in the New Jerusalem, as His royal household, to the nations as His subjects.

O. The Grace of the Lord Jesus Christ Being with the Saints

It is according to the five previous items that the grace of the Lord Jesus Christ is always with all the saints from the age of grace through the age of the kingdom to eternity for the accomplishment of the eternal economy of God.

Revelation 22:21, the last verse of the entire Bible, says, "The grace of the Lord Jesus be with all the saints. Amen." Most Christians take this verse for granted and speak in a common way about the grace of the Lord Jesus being with us. But what is the basis for saying that the grace of Christ is with us? The Lord's grace being with us is based upon all the particular aspects of the New Jerusalem. In other words, the New Jerusalem is the base upon which the grace of the Lord Jesus is with us. With the New Jerusalem as the base, the grace of the Lord Jesus is always with all the saints from the age of grace through the age of the kingdom to eternity for the accomplishment of the eternal economy of God. The grace of the Lord Jesus Christ is with us for nothing other than the accomplishing of the eternal economy of God.

ABOUT THE AUTHOR

Witness Lee was born in 1905 in northern China and raised in a Christian family. At age 19 he was fully captured for Christ and immediately consecrated himself to preach the gospel for the rest of his life. Early in his service, he met Watchman Nee, a renowned preacher, teacher, and writer. Witness Lee labored together with Watchman Nee under his direction. In 1934 Watchman Nee entrusted Witness Lee with the responsibility for his publication operation, called the Shanghai Gospel Bookroom.

Prior to the Communist takeover in 1949, Witness Lee was sent by Watchman Nee and his other co-workers to Taiwan to ensure that the things delivered to them by the Lord would not be lost. Watchman Nee instructed Witness Lee to continue the former's publishing operation abroad as the Taiwan Gospel Bookroom, which has been publicly recognized as the publisher of Watchman Nee's works outside China. Witness Lee's work in Taiwan manifested the Lord's abundant blessing. From a mere 350 believers, newly fled from the mainland, the churches in Taiwan grew to 20,000 in five years.

In 1962 Witness Lee felt led of the Lord to come to the United States, and he began to minister in Los Angeles. During his 35 years of service in the U.S., he ministered in weekly meetings and weekend conferences, delivering several thousand spoken messages. Much of his speaking has since been published as over 400 titles. Many of these have been translated into over fourteen languages. He gave his last public conference in February 1997 at the age of 91.

He leaves behind a prolific presentation of the truth in the Bible. His major work, *Life-study of the Bible,* comprises over 25,000 pages of commentary on every book of the Bible from the perspective of the believers' enjoyment and experience of God's divine life in Christ through the Holy Spirit. Witness Lee was the chief editor of a new translation of the New Testament into Chinese called the Recovery Version and directed the translation of the same into English. The Recovery Version also appears in a number of other languages. He provided an extensive body of footnotes, outlines, and spiritual cross references. A radio broadcast of his messages can be heard on Christian radio stations in the United States. In 1965 Witness Lee founded Living Stream Ministry, a non-profit corporation, located in Anaheim, California, which officially presents his and Watchman Nee's ministry.

Witness Lee's ministry emphasizes the experience of Christ as life and the practical oneness of the believers as the Body of Christ. Stressing the importance of attending to both these matters, he led the churches under his care to grow in Christian life and function. He was unbending in his conviction that God's goal is not narrow sectarianism but the Body of Christ. In time, believers began to meet simply as the church in their localities in response to this conviction. In recent years a number of new churches have been raised up in Russia and in many European countries.

OTHER BOOKS PUBLISHED BY
Living Stream Ministry

Titles by Witness Lee:

Abraham—Called by God	978-0-7363-0359-0
The Experience of Life	978-0-87083-417-2
The Knowledge of Life	978-0-87083-419-6
The Tree of Life	978-0-87083-300-7
The Economy of God	978-0-87083-415-8
The Divine Economy	978-0-87083-268-0
God's New Testament Economy	978-0-87083-199-7
The World Situation and God's Move	978-0-87083-092-1
Christ vs. Religion	978-0-87083-010-5
The All-inclusive Christ	978-0-87083-020-4
Gospel Outlines	978-0-87083-039-6
Character	978-0-87083-322-9
The Secret of Experiencing Christ	978-0-87083-227-7
The Life and Way for the Practice of the Church Life	978-0-87083-785-2
The Basic Revelation in the Holy Scriptures	978-0-87083-105-8
The Crucial Revelation of Life in the Scriptures	978-0-87083-372-4
The Spirit with Our Spirit	978-0-87083-798-2
Christ as the Reality	978-0-87083-047-1
The Central Line of the Divine Revelation	978-0-87083-960-3
The Full Knowledge of the Word of God	978-0-87083-289-5
Watchman Nee—A Seer of the Divine Revelation ...	978-0-87083-625-1

Titles by Watchman Nee:

How to Study the Bible	978-0-7363-0407-8
God's Overcomers	978-0-7363-0433-7
The New Covenant	978-0-7363-0088-9
The Spiritual Man • 3 volumes	978-0-7363-0269-2
Authority and Submission	978-0-7363-0185-5
The Overcoming Life	978-1-57593-817-2
The Glorious Church	978-0-87083-745-6
The Prayer Ministry of the Church	978-0-87083-860-6
The Breaking of the Outer Man and the Release ...	978-1-57593-955-1
The Mystery of Christ	978-1-57593-954-4
The God of Abraham, Isaac, and Jacob	978-0-87083-932-0
The Song of Songs	978-0-87083-872-9
The Gospel of God • 2 volumes	978-1-57593-953-7
The Normal Christian Church Life	978-0-87083-027-3
The Character of the Lord's Worker	978-1-57593-322-1
The Normal Christian Faith	978-0-87083-748-7
Watchman Nee's Testimony	978-0-87083-051-8

Available at
Christian bookstores, or contact Living Stream Ministry
2431 W. La Palma Ave. • Anaheim, CA 92801
1-800-549-5164 • www.livingstream.com